A'ūdhu billāhi minash-shaitānir-rajīm.
I seek refuge in Allāh from the accursed satan.

Bismillāhir-Rahmānir-Rahīm.
In the name of Allāh,
the Most Compassionate, the Most Merciful.

ISLAM
AND
WORLD
PEACE
Explanations of a SUFI

ISLAM
AND
WORLD
PEACE

Explanations of a SUFI

SECOND EDITION

M. R. Bawa Muhaiyaddeen ﵁

Fellowship Press
Philadelphia, PA

Library of Congress Control Number: 2007937600

Muhaiyaddeen, M. R. Bawa

    Islam and world peace: explanations of a sufi, second edition
        M. R. Bawa Muhaiyaddeen
        Philadelphia, PA: Fellowship Press, 2007
p. cm.
Includes index.

Trade paperback
ISBN: 978-0-914390-83-1
Hardcover
ISBN: 978-0-914390-84-8

1. Sufi 2. Islam 3. Spiritual 4. Interfaith   I. Title

Printed in the United States of America
by FELLOWSHIP PRESS
Bawa Muhaiyaddeen Fellowship
First Edition Printing 1987
Revised Edition Printing 2004
Second Edition Printing 2008

Muhammad Raheem Bawa Muhaiyaddeen ⊕

Contents

FOREWORD

◦ ✦ ◦❖◦ ✦ ◦

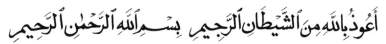
I seek refuge in Allāh from the accursed satan.
In the name of Allāh, the Most Compassionate, the Most Merciful.

Among the great religions of the world, Islam is no doubt the one that is least known and least appreciated by the non-Muslim world. The recent resurgence of military and militant groups inside Islam has caused a renewal of feelings and sentiments that have been harbored for centuries and a new spirit of crusade against the only major religion that appeared in history after Christianity. This has caused many western laymen and intellectuals to ask, "What do 'the *Islams*' have in mind now?" (A horrible form used by many instead of the correct term, *Muslims.*)

Real Islam is a deep and unquestioning trust in God, the realization of the truth that "There is no deity save God" and of the threefold aspect of religious life: that of *"Islām"*, complete surrender to God; *īmān,* unquestioning faith in Him and His wisdom, and *insān,* to do right and to act beautifully, because one knows that God is always watching man's actions and thoughts. For fourteen hundred years the Muslims have practiced these vir-

tues, and the great mystics of Islam have taught them to millions
of faithful who have survived the most difficult times, the greatest
hardships because of their unshakable faith in the loving kindness
of God, the creator, sustainer and judge of everything created.
Sufism, the mystical current inside Islam, developed logically out
of the serious study of the Koran, according to Muslim belief the
uncreated word of God, and of the constant direction of all fac-
ulties toward God. The Sufi masters taught their disciples that
their duty is the fulfillment of God's will, not out of a feeling of
duty but rather out of love—for could there be anything greater
than the unconditional love which man offers his Lord? And in
order to be able to love God and, through Him, His creatures, the
heart has to be purified by constant remembrance of God and
by constant struggle against one's lower qualities, the so-called
nafs, which are, according to a word of the Prophet of Islam,
"The greatest enemy of man." This struggle against one's lowly
and base qualities is indeed the "greater Holy War," for outward
enemies can disappear and are not as dangerous as the inner, satanic forces, which try to incite man into evil, disobedience, and
forgetfulness. It is this "Holy War" which in the following pages
forms the center of the teaching of one of the masters of Sufism
in our day, Bawa Muhaiyaddeen, who hails from Sri Lanka and
stands in the age-old tradition of wisdom and love.

The reader will learn from these pages, which are written, or
rather recited, in a simple, almost childlike style, that the inner
dimensions of Islam are very different from those which he usually associates with this religion; that there is a wealth of love,
of patience, of trust in God, and, last but not least, of gratitude,
for the qualities of patience in affliction and gratitude belong together. The true lover of God knows that even in affliction it is
the hand of the Divine Beloved that he feels, and he trusts that

whatever befalls him is for his best, for God knows what is good for the soul's growth and for the spirit's purification.

I hope that many people read the warm, loving words of Bawa Muhaiyaddeen and understand that indeed the words *islām* and *salām,* peace, belong to the same root and that a true understanding of the inner dimensions of Islam will help them to find peace for themselves, *in shā'Allāh,* God willing.

Annemarie Schimmel

Professor of Indo-Muslim Culture

Harvard University

Cambridge, Massachusetts

October, 1985

PREFACE

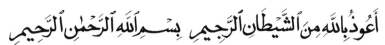

I seek refuge in Allāh from the accursed satan.
In the name of Allāh, the Most Compassionate, the Most Merciful.

To all those who, with the faith, certitude, and determination of true *īmān*, have accepted Allāh and His Rasūl ☺, it is important in this present day that we clearly understand the meaning of Islām.

To be in Islām is to have absolute faith in Allāh, to know the *Rabb*, the Almighty Lord, to bow down at His feet, pray to Him, and adopt His ways. To be in Islām is to have certitude in the messengers of God, the prophets, and the angels, and to carry out the commandments sent through them. Islām is to discard from ourselves whatever God has discarded from Himself. It is to accept Him, His three thousand gracious qualities, and His ninety-nine *wilāyats*, attributes, to bring them into our actions, and to do His service. To have this absolute faith, certitude, and determination, and to strengthen that *īmān* is the true meaning of Islām.

The children of Adam ☺ must accept Allāh and achieve clarity. They must know the value of Islām, the value of its purity and truth, its peacefulness and unity, the value of its sincerity and honesty, the value of its conscience and justice, and the greatness of Allāh who rules over all this.

Before we can come to love every life as our own life, before we can eliminate poverty, suffering, illusion, and disease in the world and bring peace to all lives, we must first understand the value of absolute faith. That is the purpose of this book.

If we claim to be in Islām, we must destroy all the evil qualities that arise within us. We must cut away and discard all the differ-ences that separate us from God. We must remove the thoughts that disrupt the unity of Adam's ☺ children, the unity of Islām. We have to fight against the separations that grow like demons and animals within our bodies and suck our blood. With the wealth of God's grace and with the help of the Rasūl ☺, we must cut away all the four hundred trillion, ten thousand evil qualities that come to destroy our good qualities.

This is the war we must wage. *Jihād*, holy war, is not some-thing to be fought on the outside. Our real enemies are within us from birth. An *insān*, a human being, will realize that it is his own evil qualities which are killing him. These are the enemies that must be conquered. We must control and subdue these animal qualities within us and keep them in their place. We must show them their true Master, Allāhu ta'ālā. We must win them over and teach them *īmān*. That is the way of Islām, and that is what this book urges us to do.

Islām is equality, peacefulness, and unity. Islām is *sabūr*, inner patience, *shukūr*, contentment, *tawakkul*, trust in God, and *al-hamdu lillāh*, all praise to God. Islām is to find tranquility in life and then to guide all lives towards that peacefulness. Islām practices the explanations given by Allāh through His revela-tions. Islām demonstrates Allāh's qualities, actions, conduct, and behavior. If a man understands this and puts it into practice, then he will be a *mu'min*, true believer. He will be Allāh's representative, one who knows Allāh and His commandments.

Allāh has given this gift of *Īmān*-Islām to those who have faith, trust, and *īmān*, to the *mu'mins*. Allāh's perfectly pure qualities, His conduct, His ninety-nine *wilāyats*, attributes, and His three thousand gracious qualities have all been gathered together with His love and made into the treasure of *Īmān*-Islām. He has given this gift to the children of Adam ☺ so that they could receive Allāh's kingdom and His wealth, and live a life filled with peacefulness. He gave this gift in abundance to the prophets, so that they could help release mankind from enslavement to earth, woman, and gold,[1] and from enslavement to desires, thoughts, and attachments. Man is a slave to so many things. He is suffering and can find no freedom. He has no peace, tranquility, equality, or love.

The children of Adam ☺ must release themselves from the sufferings that arise from this bondage. To help them do this, Allāh gave them the wealth of *sabūr, shukūr, tawakkul*, and *al-hamdu lillāh*. He gave them the wealth of His beautiful laws, His good qualities and actions and conduct, of His love and integrity. That wealth is pure and that purity is Islām. If man gains this wealth within him, he will never meet with destruction in this world or in the hereafter. He will never lack anything. He will be beautiful in both worlds. Allāh has asked mankind to accept this treasure, to free themselves, and to raise the flag of unity on the tree of love.

My brothers and sisters, we need the absolute faith, certitude,

---

1. earth, woman, and gold: This is a phrase Bawa Muhaiyaddeen ☺ often used to illustrate the underlying cause of all the fighting in the world. "Woman" is used in its singular form.

and determination of *īmān*. We must unite and live as one race, praying together as one family in one gathering, accepting that there is one God. This is the wealth of *Īmān*-Islām.

God sent this gift to all the prophets, and finally it was given in completeness to the Rasūl ☉. All that was resonated to God's messengers, they, in turn, shared with mankind, as the fundamental explanations of *īmān* in the *hadīth*, traditional stories of the prophets, in the *kitābs*, holy books, and in the Qur'ān. There are very deep meanings in these. In this book, we are only speaking in proportion to our little wisdom, the wisdom of this small man. Those with deeper wisdom may understand even deeper meanings. We are revealing to you only an atom of the value of Islām. Those who have Allāh's *'ilm*, divine knowledge, and His wisdom will find clarity from the inner meanings that lie within this book.

If there are any mistakes in what has been spoken here, please forgive me. All the children of Adam ☉, all who have *īmān* and who accept God, are one family in Islām. Therefore, please forgive me as you would forgive the mistakes of those in your own family. Please forgive me, in the name of Allāh and the Rasūl ☉.

People with wisdom know that it is important to correct their own mistakes, while people without wisdom feel it is important to point out the mistakes of others. People with strong *īmān* know that it is important to clear their own *qalbs*, inner hearts, while those with unsteady *īmān* try to find fault in the hearts and prayers of others. This becomes a habit in their lives. But those who pray to Allāh with faith, determination, and certitude know that the most important thing in life is to surrender their hearts to Allāh.

A fruit can only give the taste that it has within itself. It cannot give any other taste. In the same way, the children of Adam ☉

can only give what they have within themselves. If the pond of our heart is full, then all creations can come and partake of its clear water. But if it is shallow, then all those who come to drink from it will only stir up the mud, and all they will be able to drink is dirty water.

People with wisdom will recognize the taste of wisdom. If we have that sweetness in our own inner hearts, we will recognize that taste in others. Realizing this, if we can find Allāh and the Rasūl ☉, if we can find truth, patience, surrender, peacefulness, and tranquility within our *qalbs,* and if we can find unity among ourselves, then we will be truly exalted people.

Unity, compassion, and truth are Islām. Let us realize this and live accordingly. We are all in Islām. Allāh is sufficient for all. *Āmīn. As-salāmu ʿalaikum wa rahmatullāhi wa barakātuhu.* May the peace, the beneficence, and blessings of God be upon you. *Āmīn.*

PART ONE

PEACE

CHAPTER ONE

EVERYONE IS SPEAKING OF PEACE

As-Salām

Peace

One who has not found peace within himself will forever be giving speeches about peace. This world is a pulpit upon which man preaches, and there is no end to this talk. For millions of years man has been speaking this way, but he has not come forward to first find peace within himself.

CHAPTER ONE

EVERYONE IS SPEAKING OF PEACE

أَعُوذُ بِاللّٰهِ مِنَ الشَّيْطَانِ الرَّجِيمِ بِسْمِ اللّٰهِ الرَّحْمٰنِ الرَّحِيمِ

I seek refuge in Allāh from the accursed satan.
In the name of Allāh, the Most Compassionate, the Most Merciful.

Brothers and sisters born in this world, please listen to this wonder. The heavens and earth have always existed in peace. The sun, the moon, the stars, and the wind all perform their duty in harmony. Only man, who lives on this earth, has lost that peace. He only talks about it. He gives speeches about making peace, but then he disrupts the unity and sets out to rule the world. Is this not a wonder? Such is the speech of man.

In this present century, man has discarded God, truth, peacefulness, conscience, honesty, justice, and compassion. Man has changed so much. Instead of searching to discover the three thousand gracious qualities of God, he has lost all those good qualities and has opened the way to destruction. He seeks to ruin the lives of others and to destroy the entire world. But the world will not be destroyed. The earth and the heavens will never be destroyed; only man will be destroyed. Man, with all the various means of destruction he has discovered, will in the end destroy only himself. He is like a certain type of moth that is attracted to the glow

11

of a flame, thinking it is food. These moths circle around and around the flame, until finally they fly right into it and die. In the same way, man plummets into evil actions, thinking they will benefit him. He sees evil as good, but the end result is destruction.

Never has destruction been so much in evidence as in the present century. Man has changed the concept of God, who is Truth, and debased the meaning of man, who is wisdom and beauty. He no longer understands what a true human being really is. If man could rediscover who he truly is and then change his present self, he would know peace. Man says he wants to bring peace to others, but in order to do that, he must first find it within his own life. How can anyone who has not found peace within himself hope to bring peace to others? How can a man who has no compassion, no unity, and no love within himself bring peace to the world?

One who has not found justice, conscience, honesty, and truth within himself will not find these qualities in others. One who has not found the value of patience within himself will not find it in others. One who has not understood his own state will not understand the state of others. One who has not strengthened his own faith in God cannot strengthen the faith of others or be strengthened by the faith of others. One who has not acquired good qualities cannot find them in others, nor can he teach them to others. If he tries, his work will be fruitless. How can a man who carries a water bag full of holes hope to quench the thirst of others? As long as he has not repaired his own vessel, he can never fill that of another man.

To understand this and to establish peace, man must first change the thoughts and qualities within himself. He must change his qualities of selfishness and avarice, his desire for praise, and his love for earth, woman, and gold. He must stop thinking, "My family, my wife, my children! I must rule the world! I must advance my position in life." When a man has all these selfish ideas, how can he possibly create peace for others?

However, if he severs these qualities from himself and begins to feel the hunger, the pain, and the difficulties felt by others, and if he treats all lives as his own life, then he will find peace. If he can strive for this understanding and obtain the *sabūr,* inner patience, *shukūr,* contentment, and *tawakkulun 'alAllāh,* trust in God; if he can imbibe God's qualities and acquire God's state, then he will know peace. Once he finds that clarity within himself, he will discover peace in every life. If everyone would do this, life in this world would be heaven on earth. But if those who live in this world and rule this world cannot find serenity within themselves, they will only end up destroying the world when they try to establish peace. We must think about this.

One who has not found peace within himself will forever be giving speeches about peace. This world is a pulpit upon which man preaches, and there is no end to this talk. For millions of years man has been speaking this way, but he has not come forward to first find peace within himself. There is no use in making speeches. Man must acquire the qualities of God and live in that state. Only then can he speak of peace, only then can he speak the speech of God and dispense the justice of God's kingdom.

The people who have come to rule the world should think about this. Every man should think about this. Peace can only be found in the heart. Good qualities, wisdom, and clarity must provide that explanation within each heart. Man will only know peace when he takes God's justice and His qualities into himself. Therefore, before we speak of peace, let us try to acquire God's words within ourselves. Let us find tranquility within ourselves. If we can do that, our speech will be fruitful. Then the whole world will be at peace.

Man must find peace, tranquility, happiness, unity, love, and every good quality within his own life. Only a person who does that can understand the difficulties, the pain, and the misery of others. A man of wisdom will know this, understand this, and rectify his own mistakes. Then he can help others. We must all think about this. May God help us. *Āmīn.*

JERUSALEM
An Example for the World

Al-Qudrah

The Power of God's grace

We must use God's Power to avert the dangers and disasters that threaten mankind. If we can live with compassion and justice, then laws of truth will govern, and absolute justice will reign forever. Unity will live on, patience will be eternal, and compassion will never fail. Man must think of this. All of us must join together to bring peace to the Holy City.

CHAPTER TWO

JERUSALEM
An Example for the World

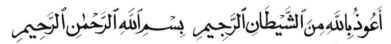

I seek refuge in Allāh from the accursed satan.
In the name of Allāh, the Most Compassionate, the Most Merciful.

The following letter was written in February, 1980, and was sent to the prominent leaders of the Middle East and the free world.

A Letter to the Leaders of the World
Who Still Have Faith in Their Hearts

May God grant His help to all our brothers and sisters who have faith. *Āmīn.*

Jerusalem is not just the name of a city. *Salām* means peace. Jerusalem is a place of peace and tranquility, but today that place of peace has become a place of conflict. We all have to reflect upon this in our own hearts. We must examine our hearts and consciences and ask ourselves, "What purpose is served by fighting and conquering lands? Does any conqueror live forever? Does anyone live forever?" We must analyze what has happened in the past and find a way to bring peace to Jerusalem.

The first part of this letter is a history of the events that took place in Jerusalem in the past, and the second part describes how we should act in the present. Please read this carefully. We write it in the hope that if we understand the history of Jerusalem, we will learn from the past and correct our mistakes, and in the hope that if we realize the futility of these continuing conflicts, we can release ourselves from the bitterness that binds us and see our rightful duty towards all mankind. We trust that each of you will read this letter with clarity in your hearts and then strive to bring peace and tranquility to the Holy City and to the world.

Please forgive me if there are any faults in what I have written. We are not attempting to present a complete history of Jerusalem; we merely want to illustrate the futility of the constant warfare and bloodshed that has plagued the Holy City. All of us must join together and bring peace to Jerusalem. May God give good qualities, peace, and wisdom to all who trust in Him. May God give these to each heart. *Āmīn.*

A CHRONOLOGICAL HISTORY OF JERUSALEM

1900 B.C.	Abraham ☺ enters Jerusalem. Melchizedek, King of Salem, welcomes and blesses him.
1300- 1240 B.C.	Moses ☺ leads the Israelites from Egypt; his followers, led by Joshua ☺, arrive in Canaan. Joshua ☺ defeats the King of Jerusalem, who is the head of the alliance of cities, but the city remains Jebusite.
1000 B.C.	David ☺ wrests Jerusalem from the Jebusites and makes it the capital of his kingdom.
970 B.C.	Solomon ☺ succeeds David ☺ as King of Israel.
950 B.C.	Solomon's Temple is completed.

928 B.C.	Shishak of Egypt sacks the city.
721 B.C.	Tiglath-Pileser of Assyria conquers northern Israel, and tiny Judea is all that remains of the empire of David ☺ and Solomon ☺.
701 B.C.	Sennacherib, King of Assyria, lays siege to Jerusalem but is repelled.
587-586 B.C.	Nebuchadnezzar of Babylon conquers Jerusalem, destroys Solomon's Temple, exiles the Jews to Babylon, and for all intents and purposes, Judea ceases to exist.
539 B.C.	Cyrus of Persia topples the Babylonian Empire, Jerusalem is freed, Nebuchadnezzar's victims are released, and the descendants of David ☺ are allowed to return to Jerusalem. Construction of the Second Temple is begun under Sheshbazzara, a descendant of the House of David ☺ and Governor of Judah, and is continued by his nephew, Zerubbabel.
515 B.C.	The rebuilt Temple of Solomon ☺ is inaugurated.
445 B.C.	Nehemiah completes the fortification of Jerusalem.
332 B.C.	Alexander the Great of Macedon conquers the Persian Empire but leaves Jerusalem untouched.
312 B.C.	After a series of battles between Alexander's generals, Ptolemy wins control over Jerusalem and takes Jewish prisoners to Alexandria.
312-198 B.C.	Rule of Ptolemaic dynasty.
198 B.C.	Antiochus III drives the Egyptians from the city.

198-169 B.C.	The Seleucids rule Jerusalem. Antiochus IV marches on Jerusalem to impose conformity of worship. The Jews are forced to conform to the Greek world and give up circumcision and their codes of cleanliness and diet. They are also forced to worship Zeus. The Temple is pillaged. Antiochus IV erects a pagan altar and sacrifices pigs before the idol of Zeus. The Scroll of the Law is torn up and burned.
164 B.C.	The Maccabees rise in rebellion and drive the Seleucids from the city and Temple. They cleanse, purify, and rededicate the Temple.
63 B.C.	Pompey and his Roman legions conquer Jerusalem. They defile the Temple and dedicate it to Imperial Rome.
40 B.C.	The Romans are driven out and the city is briefly ruled by Mattathias Antigonas, the Hasmonean king. The Romans reconquer the city.
39 B.C.	Herod is chosen by the Romans to be King of the Jews. (Herod's father was an Arab who had been forcibly converted to Judaism, and so he was readily adapted for Roman uses. Mark Antony made him a Roman citizen, and thus his son, Herod, learned Roman politics.)
20 B.C.	Construction begins on Herod's Temple.
4 B.C.	Birth of Jesus ☺. Death of Herod.
29 A.D.	Trial of Jesus ☺ and his departure from the world.
66 A.D.	Gessius Florus' troops loot the Temple's treasury, slaughtering worshippers and rabbis.

This touches off the revolt of the population of Jerusalem.

70 A.D.   Titus captures, sacks, and destroys the Second Temple. Thousands upon thousands are killed, and again Jerusalem falls into the hands of the Romans. (Six hundred and fifty-seven years after the Babylonians plundered and razed the First Temple, the Second Temple fell and none has risen since.)

132 A.D.   The Jews, led by Bar Kokhba, drive out the Romans and again make Jerusalem the Jewish capital.

135 A.D.   The Roman Emperor Hadrian destroys Jerusalem and builds on its site a city with new walls called Aelia Capitolina, with a temple on Mount Moriah dedicated to Jupiter. Hadrian bans the Jews from Jerusalem, and any Jews who defy the ban are executed.

324 A.D.   Constantine of Byzantium conquers Jerusalem.

325 A.D.   Constantine the Great embraces the Christian faith, thereby inaugurating the first Christian rule over the city. He marches under the flag of Jesus ☺, uniting the Eastern and Western Roman Empires. The city of Jerusalem is rededicated. His mother, Helena, makes a pilgrimage to Jerusalem and identifies the sites for the Church of the Holy Sepulcher and the Church of the Nativity.

336 A.D.   Constantine builds the Church of the Holy Sepulcher. (This was the rebirth of Jerusalem, both as a spiritual center and as an objective of religious pilgrimage.)

570 A.D.	Birth of Muhammad ☺.
614 A.D.	The Sassanid Persians led by Khosrau II push south through Palestine to the Sinai and Egypt, conquering Jerusalem, butchering sixty thousand Christians, selling thirty-five thousand into slavery, and demolishing the Christian shrines.
629 A.D.	The Byzantine Emperor Heraclius returns to Jerusalem, massacres the Jews, expels the survivors, and restores the ruined city.
630 A.D.	Mecca surrenders to Muhammad ☺, and during the next seven years, the empire of Heraclius begins to fall to the rising Arab nation.
632 A.D.	Death of Muhammad ☺.
638 A.D.	'Umar ibnul-Khattāb ☺, the second Muslim caliph, captures Jerusalem and builds the first mosque on the site where Solomon ☺ had erected the First Temple. 'Umar ☺ is deeply conscious of Jerusalem's universal sacredness and during his rule, there is justice and freedom of worship. As "people of the book," Christians are exempt from payment of a poll tax.
687 A.D.	'Abd al-Malik orders the erection of the Dome of the Rock (the oldest Muslim sanctuary still standing in Jerusalem) for the purpose of attracting pilgrims to the Holy City.
691 A.D.	Dome of the Rock completed. Christians and Muslims coexist peacefully and their pilgrims share the Holy City.
1077 A.D.	A fierce band of Turkish nomads called Seljuks swarm through Persia, Iraq, and Egypt, finally

seizing Jerusalem. For over twenty years the Christians are prevented from worshipping in the Holy City.

1096 A.D.   In retaliation, the first crusaders depart for the Holy Land. Their number is made up of Christians from England, France, and Germany. Over one hundred thousand foot soldiers pillage and battle their way across Asia, without order or discipline. Less than ten percent reach Jerusalem.

1098 A.D.   By the time the crusaders reach the Holy City, the Egyptians of the Fatmids Empire have recaptured the city. Though the Fatmids had always given Christians the freedom of the city, in 1099, the crusaders, led by Godfrey de Bouillon, capture Jerusalem, butchering its defendants and inhabitants, men, women, and children alike, and defile the Mosque of al-Aqsā' and the Dome of the Rock. De Bouillon becomes the Defender of the Holy Sepulcher.

1100-
1118 A.D.   Reign of Baldwin I, first ruler of the Crusader Kingdom of Jerusalem. Plaster is applied over Arabic inscriptions, and the Dome of the Rock is transformed into a Christian Church. Muslims and Jews are forbidden to reside in Jerusalem.

1187 A.D.   Saladin, Vizier of Egypt, is determined to restore the Dome of the Rock to Arab rule. Through daring political and military maneuvers, he becomes King of Egypt and Syria. Finally, he achieves his objectives and captures Jerusalem. He restores Muslim and Jewish inhabitation of the city.

1192 A.D.   Saladin and Richard the Lion-Hearted sign a

five-year truce, ending the Third Crusade and giving Christians the right to make pilgrimages to Jerusalem.

1193 A.D.   Saladin dies.

1229 A.D.   The two succeeding monarchs, the Sultan al-Kamil and Frederick II of Germany, briefly revert the Holy City to Christian rule. Warfare again sweeps the city and Jerusalem is again recaptured by the Arabs. Jerusalem would not again be governed by the Christians for nearly seven centuries.

1250 A.D.   The Mamelukes rise against the Ayyubid caliphs in Cairo, seize power in Egypt, and turn Palestine into an Egyptian province, beginning a two hundred and sixty-seven year reign of Egyptians, during which forty-seven sovereigns briefly sit upon the blood-stained throne.

1260 A.D.   The city is pillaged by the Tartars.

1267 A.D.   The Mamelukes take control of Jerusalem and inaugurate a period of architectural beautification of Muslim Jerusalem. They also rebuild the walls of the city.

1400 A.D.   The city is sacked by Genghis Khan's Mongols.

1453 A.D.   Muhammad II, a Sultan of the Ottoman Turks, successfully besieges the city of Constantinople.

1517 A.D.   Salim I (Muhammad II's grandson) captures Jerusalem from the Mameluke army. According to the original writs of 'Umar ☺, he gives the Christians jurisdiction over their holy shrines.

1537 A.D.   Suleiman the Magnificent, successor of Salim,

begins his campaign to rebuild, beautify, and fortify Jerusalem.

1816 A.D.   A decree of the reigning Sultan allows the Jews free entrance to Palestine. From this time on, the Jewish population increases rapidly.

1827 A.D.   United States opens the first diplomatic mission in Jerusalem.

1839 A.D.   British Consulate is established in Jerusalem, extending protection to the Jews.

1847 A.D.   The Catholic Church is renewed in Jerusalem.

1854 A.D.   The Crimean War is fought by Turkey, England, France, and Russia—ostensibly to settle the question of jurisdiction over Jerusalem's holy sites.

1860 A.D.   The first Jewish suburbs are built outside the walls.

1896 A.D.   Theodore Herzl publishes "The Jewish State," a pamphlet which details a plan for the establishment of an autonomous Jewish state in Palestine under the authority of the Sultan.

1897 A.D.   First Zionist Congress in Basel. The creation of a homeland for Jews in Palestine is proclaimed as the goal of the Zionist movement. There is a tremendous upsurge of Jewish migration to the Holy Land.

1917 A.D.   The British enter Jerusalem. The Ottoman army surrenders to the British. The Balfour Declaration puts Great Britain on record as favoring "a national home for the Jewish people." This declaration is then supported by France, the United States, and Italy.

1919 A.D.	The awakening Arab nationalism is voiced, with the Syrian Congress declaring its opposition to further Zionist migration.
1929 A.D.	Savage attacks on Jews in Jerusalem, Hebron, and Safad rekindle religious antagonism. The ancient Jewish communities of Safad and Hebron are almost wiped out.
1937 A.D.	Publication of the Royal (Peel) Commission, recommending the partition of Palestine.
1939–1944 A.D.	World War II. Six million Jews are killed by the Germans. British government issues White Paper in 1939, limiting immigration of Jewish refugees.
1945 A.D.	Germany surrenders and thirty thousand Jews are released from Nazi concentration camps.
1946 A.D.	Underground, illegal immigration to Israel of Jewish survivors of the German concentration camps commences.
1947 A.D.	United Nations votes partition of Palestine and creates Israel as the new Jewish state.
1948 A.D.	British withdraw from Palestine. The state of Israel is proclaimed with Jerusalem as its capital. War engulfs the area. Jerusalem is partitioned.
1951 A.D.	King 'Abdullah of Transjordan, early advocate of Arab confederation, is assassinated in the Mosque al-Aqsā'.
1956 A.D.	War. The Sinai Campaign.
1967 A.D.	Six-Day War: Israelis seize Golan Heights, Sinai, Gaza, the West Bank, and Old Jerusalem from the Arabs. The city is under Israeli rule.

1973 A.D.   Yom Kippur War.

1979 A.D.   Israel and Egypt reach a peace agreement. A
timetable is set for returning captured lands. The
process of returning the lands and normalization
of relationship is begun.

1980 A.D.   Jerusalem Basic Law enacted declaring united
Jerusalem to be capital of Israel.

1981 A.D.   President Anwar Sadat of Egypt assassinated.

1994 A.D.   Mutual recognition of Israel and the Palestinian
Authority. Warren Christopher, the United States
Secretary of State, visits Chairman Yasir Arafat
and the Palestinian National Council—the first
of more than a dozen trips by United States
Secretaries of State. Jordan and Israel sign a peace
treaty calling for close economic and political
cooperation.

1995 A.D.   Israeli Prime Minister Yitzhak Rabin assassinated
by an ultra-nationalist Israeli opposed to Rabin's
Land-for-Peace agreements with the Palestinians.

1998 A.D.   President Bill Clinton persuades Israeli Prime
Minister Netanyahu to allow United States
involvement in security negotiations. President
Clinton addresses Palestinian Authority.

1999 A.D.   Talks between Israeli Prime Minister Ehud Barak
and Syrian Foreign Minister Farouk al-Sharaa
begin in Washington D.C.

2000 A.D.   President Clinton convenes intensive peace
talks at Camp David between Israel and the
Palestinians. Talks collapse. Ariel Sharon, prior
to his election as Prime Minister of Israel, visits

one of the holiest sites in Jerusalem, the Temple Mount, also known as Haram al-Sharif. A second Palestinian *intifada* quickly follows.

2001 A.D.   Intense peace talks between Egypt and Israel end without an agreement. International commission headed by former United States Senator George Mitchell submits a report calling for an end to the violence. Both sides accept the report but with different interpretations. United States CIA Director George Tenet works with both sides to implement the Mitchell plan, but the effort stalls.

2002 A.D.   United States Secretary of State Colin Powell concludes a ten-day trip to the Middle East without securing a cease-fire between the Palestinian Authority and the Israelis. The Arab League meets to present a plan for peace in the region. The Saudi peace plan is unveiled. Secret talks between Israeli intelligence and Palestinian officials take place. A new Palestinian cabinet is established under Arafat.

2003 A.D.   Continuation of secret peace talks. Mahmoud Abbas becomes prime minister. Bush Road Map to peace is published. Summit in Aqaba bringing together Bush, Sharon, Abbas. Death of Edward Said, an advocate of the Palestinian cause in America. Egyptian Foreign Minister attacked by Palestinians in visit to Haram al-Sharif/Temple Mount.

2004 A.D.   Death of Yasir Arafat.

2005 A.D.   Mahmoud Abbas elected President of Palestinian Authority. Israeli withdrawal from Gaza (sum-

mer). Sharon and Peres form a new party
(November).

2006 A.D.   Fighting in northern Israel/southern Lebanon.
Ariel Sharon suffers a stroke, becomes incapaci-
tated. Ehud Olmert becomes Prime Minister.

2007 A.D.   Diplomatic shuttling by United States Secretary
of State Condoleeza Rice.[1]

These wars and miseries have afflicted Jerusalem since the
time of Abraham ☺. Similar incidents occurred even earlier,
right from the time of Adam ☺. Jerusalem should be a sacred
shrine, a common place of worship where the entire human race
can express their faith in God. As proof of this, from the time
of Adam ☺, God sent various prophets to the world to witness
that there is one God, but in every country where the prophets
delivered this message, the people only became divided among
themselves. Some believed in religion but did not believe in God.
Some clung to racial differences but did not cling to God.

However, there were those who did have faith in God and
in religion. There were even a few who accepted God and all the
prophets and believed that all people were the children of Adam ☺.
But the majority only sought titles and positions without accepting God or the truth. They were ready to conquer lands for the
sake of gold, property, and wealth, but they would not accept the
words of God, His compassion, His mercy, or the quality of caring
for other lives as they cared for their own. They refused to nurture
God's compassionate qualities or to accept the kingdom of love

---

1. This chronological history was reviewed and updated by Muhammad Abdul
Lateef Hayden and Rabbi Judd Kruger Levingston, Ph.D.

which encompasses compassion, mercy, tolerance, and equality. Instead they accepted satan, worldly possessions, and properties. They ruled their kingdoms with selfishness, preferring to worship satan, animals, snakes, scorpions, and spirits, and trusting in the miracles of spirits, demons, earth, fire, water, air, the sun and the moon, and maya, illusion. They believed in the power of these miracles and used them to try to destroy God, faith in God, and the truth, equality, and peace of God.

The history of Jerusalem exemplifies the state of the entire world. It is a testimony to the constant fighting from the time of Adam ☺ until now. We who belong to the human race must heed this example and learn from it.

All those who captured Jerusalem in the past shed the blood of so many human beings, cutting off heads and hands and indulging in other evil actions of cruelty and violence. We have witnessed these bloodbaths from then until now. God sent the prophets to the world to establish the word of God, His laws of justice and righteousness, His peacefulness and tolerance, His compassion for all lives, and the actions of His ninety-nine powers. He sent the prophets with His word to establish compassion in the hearts of the people. They came to develop unity and faith in God, so that the human race would live as one family, accepting one God, the Day of Judgment, and the laws of God. For this purpose, God sent 124,000 prophets in all. Twenty-five of them are mentioned in the Qur'ān. Their stories are also recounted in the Bible and the Torah.

If the human race had realized the meaning of God's message, they would not have indulged in the frenzy of wars which have resulted in rivers of blood and the destruction of lives. Even though wars have been fought throughout the entire world during the past two hundred million years (in all four yugas), they have been especially concentrated in this central point of the world—in Jerusalem. This city, which should have been a place where people from all countries could congregate in unity, has been turned into a battlefield. All of us must understand this. Every person of every religion who has seen this sacrifice of human life, this murder of human life, and these rivers of blood, must realize what is happening. The story of Jerusalem is the history of the world.

If we ever hope to live as one human race, we must have absolute faith in God. This is our only treasure. We must live according to justice and conscience, respecting the lives and bodies of all others as we do our own, and knowing the hunger and the suffering of others as our own hunger and suffering. If human beings of all four religions would realize this and live as one in unity, then these places of worship would not be turned into battlefields. It is necessary for people of all races and nationalities to realize this.

Those who came to rule Jerusalem in years gone by are no longer alive. It does not matter whether they conquered Jerusalem or Egypt or the entire world. Today these rulers are not here. Even the land itself has changed. Part of the land has been lost to the sea, and some places which the sea once covered have again become land. Where forests once stood, cities have arisen and ancient cities are now buried under forests. Cemeteries have become cities, and cities have turned into cemeteries. Over the centuries, many parts of the world have been destroyed by the sea, by wind, by rain, by fire, and by earthquakes.

We have related the history of Jerusalem to show that all those who ruled there throughout the ages have moved on, and that whoever rules there now will also ultimately move on. This is the truth. Therefore, in this one place which all four religions honor, let us establish what is unchanging. Let us come together as one and have faith in the one God and worship Him. We who are born as human beings must accept the words of the prophets, the commandments of God, and the laws of unity. We must bring clarity to our faith, to our wisdom, and to our peace.

Allāhu taʿālā Nāyan, Almighty God, is the very form of compassion. He may be called by any name in any language: God, Āndavan, Rahmān, Adōnai, Allāh, or Yahweh, but He is still the one God. All the religions of the human race must realize this. May each of us understand it, and may each of us cut any thoughts of divisiveness from our hearts.

The Arab countries, the United States, Canada, Israel, France, England, Australia, and the African countries must think about the state of the world today. They must reflect on the state and fate of Jerusalem. The age of destruction has now dawned. We are approaching a third world war. Groups have emerged which represent the antichrist, *dajjāl*. They live trusting in the world, and they lose faith in God as soon as they encounter sorrow. They indulge in selfish acts, ruling as dictators and causing much suffering.

Many groups like this have arisen in the world. They have set out to capture the world and destroy the people who have faith in God. One group who denies the existence of God has joined hands with other groups who, because of poverty, have lost their faith in God. The nature of their rule is to reign with guns and turn the world into rivers of blood. Ever since such people first emerged, they have entered different lands, spreading their false propaganda, destroying faith in God, and eventually conquering the people.

All the countries that have faith in God, the countries which have compassion and feeling, must reflect on this. Those without faith in God are creeping in and entering wherever faith in God still exists. They are trying to divide lands, disrupt the peace of the people, and create poverty—all under the false promise of peace and stability. They creep into countries, destroying everything that is good, fostering everything that is evil, bringing torment to all lives, tearing bodies apart, and creating untold suffering. Such is the state of the world in this century.

￤ All the countries that have faith in God must unite. Those who have conscience, those who have justice and wisdom and compassion in their hearts, and those who have tried to create peace among human beings must unite to bring peace to the people of the world. Once united, we must search out hardship wherever it exists and attempt to alleviate the suffering that accompanies it.

The larger countries where faith in God still prevails, such as England, France, the United States, Canada, and Australia, must unite and carry out the laws of justice. We must discover the areas that have already been infiltrated by these agents who have no faith in God, agents whom many countries are now willing to follow. This is why world peace, unity, compassion, and goodness are in danger of being lost. Therefore, it has become necessary for the countries that still have faith in God and His justice to consider this. If you examine the history of what has happened in Jerusalem, you will realize how urgent and necessary this is.

If all of us join together in the name of faith and in a state of equality, wisdom, and justice, if we can pluck out that root of evil through which all destruction occurs, and if we can show the countries of the world a path whereby all can live in unity and peace, these poisonous germs will lose their ability to infect new areas, and many countries of the world will find peace. Then these evil winds and poisonous germs capable of destroying the good crops will not be able to reach their target. These evil forces and their poisonous qualities will lose their power.

If all of us will reflect on this, if the leading figures in the United Nations and in the governments of all the larger nations will join together and try to discover where that poisonous needle has penetrated and then extract it, only then will the countries that still have faith in God find some peace.

The root of this evil must be found and removed. Then peace will flourish among the people of the world. Justice will prevail, as it did before. Honesty and integrity will rise again, and the people will live in a state of lasting peace. The larger countries, the Arab countries, Israel, and the other countries that still have faith in God must think of this and remove the needle through which these poisonous germs have been injected into the people.

The United States, England, and many other countries have engaged in wars before, but they have always shown compassion and returned the conquered countries to independent rule, allowing them to live in freedom. They have helped to avert the wars which would have come to these lands, and they have protected them in times of danger.

When the colonists first came to America more than two hundred years ago, they encountered great hardship. Remembering this, the United States must realize that this same hardship may come to people of other countries. The British Empire grew far and wide, extending from sunrise to sunset, but now those colonies have been returned to their own people, and England has returned to her own shores. But today an evil germ has crept in among those countries and continually creates trouble. This faction, which denies the existence of God, is greedily attempting to capture and plunder other lands.

When Germany attacked Russia, the Allied Nations joined to defeat Germany and protect Russia. The Allied Nations then freed the countries which they occupied during the war, but they (the communists) did not. Ruling by the gun and forcing people to obey, they enslaved countries and compelled them to do as they were told, without protest. And today it (communism) continues to rule over countries, imposing its values and its government upon them, denying them any freedom. Still not satisfied, it wants to expand its dominion even further. It clings to what it has and seeks to capture more and more. For its own gain, it disrupts the unity of the world.

All nations and all people must realize that each of the prophets came to release us from the tyranny of those who have no faith in God and who deny His existence. The prophets came to release us from the grasp of poverty and the slavery of the soul. They came to release us from satan, from illusion, from the bondage of our body, and from the bondage of governments. The prophets did release us from all these forces of slavery and gave us a place to live in freedom and unity, did they not?

Thinking back on all that has happened to us, we must be aware of the plight of others. We are not different from other people. If we remember our own suffering, we will find it easy to live without causing suffering now. To live together in unity as brothers and sisters is a sign of the children who accept God and who will rule the kingdom of God. The people of Israel, Egypt, the Arab nations, the United States, and all countries must reflect deeply on this. We must understand the suffering of others, and avoid causing suffering to each other. We must act with compassion and love, following what our conscience tells us is good. We must strive to allow everyone to live in freedom and peace.

There is one other problem, which the larger nations need to focus their attention upon. On the very day that an amicable settlement is achieved between the Palestinians and Israel, world peace will be assured, all divisiveness will be erased, world wars will stop, and world destruction will be halted. The only hope for peace in that area lies in convincing these two groups to live as peaceful neighbors and in establishing a United Nations Peace Force to maintain border security between the two lands.

If we assure these two groups that they can live in peace and unity, we will have removed the basic cause of dissatisfaction.

Look at Jerusalem. How many people have ruled, how many wars have been fought, how many people have been enslaved, how much danger and suffering there has been. If we can understand all this and bring peace to Jerusalem, then all the enemies of those who have faith in God will be struck down. Religious differences will disappear, and all those who believe in God can live in unity. Enmity will cease if those with no faith in God and those who reject God can be kept out of Jerusalem, and if people of all religions who worship and have faith in one God will realize that lack of faith in God is the root of all this enmity. On that very day, battles will stop. There will be no more murders, no more bloodbaths. All differences will be cut away.

Each one of you, the United Nations, America, Europe, the Arab countries, Israel, England, the African countries, and all others who trust in God must realize this basic cause of enmity and cut it away. I say this because the war of destruction seems to be imminent, and I can see where the enemy is. All must join in unity, now.

God accepts Jews, Christians, and Muslims alike, and all are found in Jerusalem. Yet all the fighting is over Jerusalem. Those who have faith in God as well as those who do not have faith in God have engaged in battle. This has only resulted in destruction. Each conqueror reigned for a short time and then left the kingdom to his successor. Please reflect on this and realize that other than God all else will change. Everything in this world changes; only God remains the same forever. There have been many who have ruled the earth and many who have ruled the countryside, but they are all gone. And there are still more to come who will rule and then pass on. No one can rule forever. We must be aware of this truth.

If mankind will realize this, then we can avert disaster by coming together with faith in God and living in unity and compassion. Do not live divided. With compassion for each other, live in unity and truth, in the presence of God. Let there be unity among mankind. Have *sabūr,* patience, *shukūr,* contentment, *tawakkulun 'alAllāh,* trust in God, and *al-hamdu lillāh,* all praise is to God. Live praising God at all times, and peace will be easy.

It is not customary for me to speak about politics. But when I look at what is happening now, I see the world threatened by the danger of atomic energies and the arrogance of human beings. I see how much suffering is being caused by the obstinacy and selfishness of mankind. And I see that it will end in destruction.

This state is fast approaching, and all of us will die. We must realize this and take the proper steps to avert disaster before the bombs start falling. Very soon those bombs might fall and burst in our hands. But if we can establish a state of peace, we might gain victory over destruction.

All these things have happened before, and they are happening again. And to what purpose? We must live in unity as one human race, worship one God, and fashion laws of righteousness and justice which will take us back to our Creator. That will provide exaltedness to our lives. That will elevate our lives.

We must all attain this state. This is why I most humbly ask all of you to try to avert the disaster that threatens us. We must escape from this imminent destruction. If we live without the differences of "I" and "you," we can escape from the evil of destruction in this world. Instead of trying to cure these ills with the arrogance that thinks, "We are greater than they are!" we must cure them by using the qualities of God and the tolerance of God. We must use God's Power to avert the dangers and disasters that threaten mankind. If we can live with compassion and justice, then true laws will govern, and absolute justice will reign forever. Unity will live on, patience will be eternal, and compassion will never fail. Man must think about this.

All of us must join together to bring peace to the Holy City.

May God give His grace, the wealth of the three worlds, undiminishing life, and peace without any sorrow to my loving brothers and sisters, to those who are older than I, to those who are younger than I, and to all who have been born with me. *Āmīn.*

I am writing this letter to show how peace could be brought to the world. Everyone with wisdom and faith must realize this, and if we who are the human generation can bring such peace to fruition, then we can reach exaltedness in our lives. I am saying this out of the awareness which comes from my heart. This is not being said to attack anyone, to find fault with anyone, or to show differences towards anyone. If there are any faults in what I have said, please forgive me. If there are mistakes in this letter, I am asking everyone who reads it to please forgive me. *Āmīn.* Allāh is sufficient unto all. *Āmīn.*

CHAPTER THREE

JUSTICE FOR ALL
Hadīth of
ʿUmar ibnul-Khattāb ﷺ

Mu'min

A true believer

If we are *mu'mins,* true believers, we will not see any differences between others and ourselves. We will see only One. We will see Allāh, one human race, and one justice for all. That justice and truth is the strength of Islām. That compassion and peace is the strength of Islām.

CHAPTER THREE

JUSTICE FOR ALL
Hadīth of 'Umar ibnul-Khattāb ﷺ

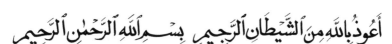

I seek refuge in Allāh from the accursed satan.
In the name of Allāh, the Most Compassionate, the Most Merciful.

We have spoken of the flag of Islām, the flag of *īmān*, the tree of faith, and the Power of Allāh. It is through this pure faith, this *īmān*, that we must establish the connection of our pure heart with Allāh and pray to Him. This is necessary for all those in Islām.

There is a *hadīth*, a traditional story, about 'Umar ibnul-Khattāb ﷺ, the Islamic caliph who took over the city of Jerusalem and the sacred sanctuary now known as al-Baitul-Muqaddas.[1]

'Umar ﷺ was a ruler of great justice and peace. He was given the beautiful name of Amīrul-Mu'minīn, the Commander of the Faithful, because of his noble qualities, and it was his rightful duty to receive the key to this Holy City which was the original *qiblah*, the direction Muslims face while praying.

The armies of 'Umar ﷺ had already entered Jerusalem and

---

1. al-Baitul Muqaddas: The original temple in Jerusalem over which is now built the Masjidul-Aqsā' and near which site the Dome of the Rock stands today.

41

taken control of the city from the Christians who had ruled there since the time of Constantine. When 'Umar ☺ came to take official possession of Jerusalem, he came alone. He journeyed from Damascus to Jerusalem with only one camel and a cameleer. The caliph, being a man of great humility, had arranged with the cameleer that they would both take turns riding the camel. According to justice, he would ride for a while, then the cameleer would ride and he would walk.

Meanwhile, the entire city was awaiting 'Umar's ☺ impending arrival. The bishop of the Holy Sepulcher had announced, "The great Islamic leader is coming! We must greet him and pay our respects to him." So all the people had gathered at the city gate, awaiting the grand royal procession. But no procession appeared.

Instead, after a while, two people became visible on the horizon, approaching very slowly. When they finally reached the city, it was the cameleer's turn to be riding, and so all the people mistook him for the caliph and rushed to greet him.

"Wait! I am not the caliph," the cameleer said, and he explained their arrangement to take turns riding and walking. The people, overwhelmed by this justice, praised the great caliph.

The bishop was also amazed by such justice. His heart filled with joy, and he handed the key of the city to 'Umar ibnul-Khattāb ☺.

The bishop then invited 'Umar ☺ to perform his prayers within their church. When 'Umar ☺ saw the interior decorated with all the Christian symbols, he politely declined, saying, "I will pray just outside your doors."

Once he had finished, the bishop asked, "Why would you not come inside our church?"

"If I had prayed in your sanctuary," 'Umar ☺ explained, "my

followers and those who come here in the future would take over this building and turn it into a mosque. They would destroy your place of worship. To avoid these difficulties and allow your church to continue as it is, I prayed outside."

Again the bishop was amazed by his justice. "Today, because of your justice, faith, wisdom, and truth, you have received the key to this Holy City. But for how long will this remain in your hands? When will this sacred place come back into our possession?"

'Umar ibnul-Khattāb ☺ replied, "Today we have indeed taken over this place of worship with *īmān*, wisdom, justice, and truth. It is with these four qualities that we have regained this city. As long as these four exist in Islām, as long as the Muslims have all four in their hands, they will retain the city. But when these qualities depart from Islām, this place of worship will change hands once again.

"If it happens that we must lose this place to someone else, it will be because we lack certitude in our faith. When the Muslims sell the truth and collect worldly wealth and seek worldly pleasures; when they lose good faith, good conduct, and the good behavior of modesty and reserve; when they relate to women in an immoral and unjust way; when they behave with backbiting, jealousy, and envy; when they lack unity and establish hypocrisy; when they destroy good deeds and degenerate into committing evil actions—when all this occurs in the midst of Islām, then unity and peacefulness will be destroyed. These evil qualities and actions will cause divisions and separations, and this Holy City will be taken from our hands. That is certain.

"When this happens, the followers of Islām will be as numerous as the granules of flour in dough. But the number of those who shall take possession of the city will be as few as the grains of salt in the dough. This will happen when degradation permeates Islām."

These were the words of 'Umar ibnul-Khattāb ☻ when he took possession of the Holy City and the sacred ground of al-Baitul-Muqaddas.

My brethren, we have to understand the state of Islām today and reflect upon the words of 'Umar ibnul-Khattāb ☻. We must realize that if man wants peace and justice in the world and in his life, then he himself must conduct his life with these qualities. That is the only way man will find peace anywhere. Islām and the human society must realize this.

Each one of us should reflect and understand within himself what he must do. He must develop his faith, certitude, and determination. Each person must look within himself, find clarity, strengthen his *īmān*, his faith, certitude, and determination, and raise that benevolent flag of Islām in his life.

When 'Umar ibnul-Khattāb ☻ was given the key to the Holy City, he spoke about four essential things which must always exist in Islām: truth, justice, wisdom, and certitude. As long as Islām retains these four and lives in unity, comforting with compassion and giving peace to other lives, there will be peace in Islām. But when this justice changes, peace will be lacking. The time is now approaching when we will find no peace in Islām or in the hearts of the people. We must think about this.

Before the time of Muhammad ☻, the Arab nations underwent tremendous difficulties. There was so much poverty, famine, and sorrow. Then through the *du'ā' barakah* of the Rasūlullāh ☻, because of his pleading for God's blessing, these countries received the amazing wealth of *īmān*. The light of Islām burned in every house. The undiminishing wealth of *sabūr,* inner patience, *shukūr,* contentment, *tawakkul,* trust in God, and *al-hamdu lillāh,* all praise to God, filled every *qalb*. Through the *duʿāʾ barakah* of the Prophet ☺, Allāhu taʿālā changed the desert into *rahmah*, grace. Where there was not even water to drink, He made oil, and that oil was converted into gold and jewels. This happened because of the prayers and blessings of the Rasūlullāh ☺, because of the richness of *īmān*.

God poured endless wealth into the desert where nothing would grow and gave it to the community of Islām, and that wealth still exists there today. Allāhu taʿālā gave them this because of their *īmān*, did He not? If the community of Islām forfeits their treasure of *īmān*, then those earthly treasures will be lost. You and I should realize this.

In another *hadīth*, the Rasūlullāh ☺ said, "Do not waste your fortune, do not waste your money, do not throw away your wealth, do not waste anything. Instead, share it with your brothers. Help your brothers, take care of them, and take care of your relatives. Do not be wasteful." We who are *Īmān*-Islām must understand this today. If all the leaders, the *ʿulamāʾ*, the shaikhs, and the *sayyids* understood this, no one would be poor in Islām.

Allāh has said that kings and beggars must pray to Him side by side, embrace each other heart to heart, give *salāms*, greetings of peace, at each *waqt*, time of prayer, and thus show the unity of Islām. He said that everyone accepted by the Qurʾān must be shown unity. And since the Qurʾān does not perceive differences among people, everyone in the world must be accepted. Nothing can be found in the words of the Qurʾān that indicates showing differences among people.

The Qurʾān speaks of twenty-five prophets, including Adam, Noah, Abraham, Ishmael, Moses, David, Jesus, Idris, Isaac, Job, Sālih, Joseph, Jonah, and other prophets like them, may the peace of Allāh be upon them all. The *nabīs*, prophets, the *auliyāʾ*, saints, the *malā'ikah,* archangels, and the *qutbs,* the great holy men of divine wisdom, are all spoken of in the *hadīth* and in the other holy books:

Lā ilāha illAllāhu Ādam Safīullāh.
There is no God but Allāh. Adam is the pure one of Allāh.

Lā ilāha illAllāhu Nūhun Najīyullāh.
There is no God but Allāh. Noah is the one saved by Allāh.

Lā ilāha illAllāhu Ibrāhīm Khalīlullāh.
There is no God but Allāh. Abraham is the friend of Allāh.

Lā ilāha illAllāhu Ismā'īl Dhabīhullāh.
There is no God but Allāh. Ishmael is the sacrifice of Allāh.

Lā ilāha illAllāhu Mūsā Kalīmullāh.
There is no God but Allāh. Moses is the one who
spoke with Allāh.

Lā ilāha illAllāhu Dāwūd Khalīfatullāh.
There is no God but Allāh. David is the vice-regent of Allāh.

Lā ilāha illAllāhu 'Īsā Rūhullāh.
There is no God but Allāh. Jesus is the soul of Allāh.

Lā ilāha illAllāhu Muhammadur-Rasūlullāh,
sallallāhu 'alaihi wa sallam.
There is no God but Allāh. Muhammad is His Messenger, may
Allāh bless him and grant him peace.

Allāh sent down each of the prophets and directed them to preach His commandments. Their message came from His resonance. He alone sent them the *wahys,* revelations, and gave them the words. Therefore, we must not see the prophets as differing from each other; they should only be seen in unity, as one. Allāh does not reject any of them.

The Qur'ān does not show hatred towards any religion; it accepts them all as paths leading to the One. Can we then reject any of these teachings, considering them separate from ourselves? No, we must take everything accepted by the Qur'ān into our hearts. We are told in the Qur'ān to accept what is accepted by God and to discard what is discarded by God. Satan, alcohol, drugs, falsehood, jealousy, anger, sins, the arrogance of the "I," and other evil qualities and actions like these are discarded by the Qur'ān. They are all opposed by the Qur'ān, by Allāh, and by the *rasūls,* the messengers of God, and therefore should also be discarded by the heart of an *insān,* a human being. That heart is the true Qur'ān and should be a place where only *īmān* and love for Allāh dwell. *Insān* should accept only Allāh's duties, Allāh's commands, and the resonance of the Qur'ān. That is justice and that is Islām.

But think about what we are doing now. If we understood and accepted the words of the Rasūlullāh ⊕ and the words of the Qur'ān, we would not consider anyone our enemy; we would not fight with anyone. We should not see any differences or cause any opposition. Everyone who accepted God would be our brothers; only those who denied God would be our enemies. This is what the Qur'ān points out. No matter what religion or scripture or prophet people may follow, all are the children of Adam ⊕, all belong to the family of Abraham ⊕. They are our brothers and followers of the Rasūl ⊕. There is one sun and one moon. They do not show any differences towards the things they shine upon. When the rain falls, does it fall on one thing and not another? When the wind blows, does it show any differences? No, it blows the same way for all. Does the earth show preferences? Does water show any differences or separations?

In the same way, Islām must not see any differences between one life and another. Like the sun and the moon, Islām should perform its duty and show its love to everyone alike. The sun showers its brilliant rays upon the whole world, and the moon gives its cooling light, dispelling the darkness. In the same way, Islām should dispel the dark torpor of evil, cool the hearts, and give love.

Allāh gave man this benevolent umbrella of Islām, the umbrella of *rahmah,* grace. To have equality, justice, compassion, unity, tranquility, and peace—this is Islām. Division is not Islām. Truth, compassion, and unity are Islām. Tranquility and peace are Islām. To end the worries of all lives and to embrace all lives is Islām. This is the message of the Qur'ān, the treasure that came from the resonance of Allāh. Islām should understand this. These were the instructions, the truths, and the justice given to the *rasūls,* messengers of God.

O brothers and sisters, think about this. This same truth can be found in the *hadīth,* which we have already spoken about. We can understand many things from them. On the outside, they are stories, but when we examine them with wisdom and *īmān,* we can see the real meaning inside. Just as there is a difference between the inside and outside of a mirror, a difference exists in everything that the eyes can see. A snake looks beautiful on the outside, but it is full of poison inside. Shape and color are on the outside of fruit and other foods, but there is taste on the inside. Some things may look beautiful but have no taste, while others may look ugly but be very tasty. It is also like this in the *'ilm,* divine knowledge, that we learn, in the wisdom that we learn, in the qualities and actions that we learn, and in the body. Differences exist between the outside and the inside of everything. Therefore, we must look at both in order to understand the meaning.

However, true Islām is the same on the inside and the outside. Its actions are the same inside and out. Its justice and its speech are the same. We must understand this. Allāh is the only One who is not hidden by any outer covering. Neither is Islām hidden by anything. A light which has nothing blocking it is pure light. The word that has no envy is a true word. That which shows no differences is love. True unity does not distinguish between high and low. True compassion considers all lives as its own and does duty without showing preferences. True justice is to act without the difference of "mine and yours." Conscience is to realize one's own faults rather than looking at the faults of others. It is to understand the state of another and say, "If I were in his place, would I not have done this also? If I had been in his state of poverty, I too might have stolen and lied the way he did. Therefore, I share in his guilt." Having understood this, we must show *sabūr*, inner patience, and *shukūr*, contentment. We must realize why that man acted as he did, and comfort him, give him love, help him to be peaceful, and bring him to the good path. That is Islām. That is what is called conscience.

Like this, in every way we have to look at our own faults and understand others' faults. Then we must correct our faults and give peace to the others. If we are *mu'mins*, true believers, we will not see any differences between others and ourselves. We will see only One. We will see Allāh, one human race, and one justice for all. That justice and truth is the strength of Islām. That compassion and peace is the strength of Islām. That unity gives strength and peace to man in this life and in *ākhirah*, the hereafter. That is *Īmān*-Islām. Islām is Allāh's good gift. It is the completeness and resplendence that gives peace to all lives. It is love, grace, unity, and compassion. It is to live as one race and one family. That is Islām.

It is this that conquers the world by conquering every heart with love. It is compassion that conquers. It is unity that conquers. It is Allāh's good qualities, behavior, and actions that conquer others. It is this state that is called Islām. The sword does not conquer. Love is sharper than the sword. It is an exalted, gentle sword.

My brethren, peacefulness and equality are greater than anger. Instead of gaining victory by fighting, use the sword of patience. That is the best way to receive Allāh's wealth. Try to understand the outside and know the inside. Then you will receive that good gift of Īmān-Islām. As long as this state does not develop within us, it is certain that destruction will occur. The life of man and the dunyā, world, will both be destroyed. However, if we conduct ourselves with the qualities of Allāh, then Islām will never reach a low state and truth will never decline. Goodness will not decline. The kingdom of Allāh's justice will always be kept in His hand. The kingdom of heaven and the kingdom of truth and justice will be in His hand as long as we hold onto these good qualities and actions. This world will be ākhirah, and our life here will be a life in heaven, a life of grace. That is certain. This is true Islām. These are Allāh's words, given in His commandments and revelations, and in the hadīth that were given to the Rasūl ☺. May we in Islām think about this.

This is the certitude of the heart of Bawa Muhaiyaddeen. Please forgive us if there are any mistakes or faults.

As-salāmu ʿalaikum wa rahmatullāhi wa barakātuhu kulluhu. May all the peace, the beneficence, and the blessings of God be upon you. Āmīn.

CHAPTER FOUR

PEACE CAN ONLY BE FOUND IN GOD

Ad-Daulah

The wealth of God

God's wealth is all you need for your life and for the resplendence of your soul. Until you understand this, you will know only disturbances in your life. Even if you rule the world, obtain titles and status, and acquire great treasures, gold, and land, you will never find peace. The only peace you can find is in God, in His qualities, His actions, His justice, His compassion, His patience, and His unity.

PEACE CAN ONLY BE FOUND IN GOD

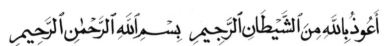

أَعُوذُ بِاللهِ مِنَ ٱلشَّيْطَانِ ٱلرَّجِيمِ، بِسْـــمِ ٱللهِ ٱلرَّحْمٰنِ ٱلرَّحِيمِ

I seek refuge in Allāh from the accursed satan.
In the name of Allāh, the Most Compassionate, the Most Merciful.

As-salāmu 'alaikum wa rahmatullāhi wa barakātuhu kulluhu. May all the peace, the beneficence, and the blessings of God be upon you.

For those of us who have faith in God alone, there is only one teaching. Whatever religion we belong to, whether it be Hinduism, Zoroastrianism, Christianity, Judaism, or Islām, and whatever prayers we say, what is it that we are really searching for? Only one thing—that Treasure which is God. Those who have no faith need many things in this world. They find satisfaction in unjust actions, political disturbances, jealousy, deceit, selfishness, and pride. But those who search for these things will never find peace or equality. They lead a life without unity, justice, or peace. That is their hell, and they make this endless hell their life.

However, any society that recognizes the one God and holds nothing equal to Him, any society that holds onto that one Truth, worshipping Him, praying to Him, and surrendering to Him— any society that has reached that state of understanding needs

53

only one Master. The people of such a society need only God, His
qualities, His actions, His conduct, His grace, His patience, and
His compassion. What else is there that matters?

All who have faith in God are striving and searching for the
same thing. Therefore, we must have no divisions of race, religion, or caste, for wherever there are separations, we can never
see God. Only in the place where no divisions exist can one see
God. These divisions keep us apart from His qualities, from His
grace, from His treasure, from His justice, from His knowledge,
and from His truth and peace. They separate us from God. Those
who have such differences within will never find peace.

We must realize that the human society is one. We are all the
children of Adam ☻, and there is only one God and one prayer.
The Bible, the Hindu Purānas, the Zend-Avesta, the Torah, and
the Qur'ān—all these scriptures contain the words of grace given
by God to the prophets. That grace is light. If you look at these
scriptures on the outside, you will see only a book, nothing more.
If you look inside, you will find pages, letters, words, sentences,
and stories. But if you look within those, you will find Allāh, the
words of Allāh, the duties of the prophets, the commandments,
the Power, the Light.

Allāh placed all these explanations inside man and told him
to look at them with understanding. This vast treasure contains
His three thousand gracious qualities, His ninety-nine wilāyats,
actions, His justice and peacefulness, heaven, hell, and the world.
Allāh made this the qalb of insān, the heart of man, and placed a
light within it. Having placed this light inside, He then explained
it on the outside through the scriptures. God has said to insān,
"Your body is a book, and your heart is a heaven. Your wisdom
is a resplendent light, and I am the Power within that wisdom.
The qalb of insān is My kingdom, the kingdom which I rule. This

is My history and your history. When you understand this, you will live in unity. You will be My 'abd, My slave, and I will be your Master. Then I can give you whatever you need and make you peaceful."

Therefore, when you study the Qur'ān and other scriptures, take the inner meaning, place it deep inside, look at it with understanding, and then speak the words of God with God, who is your wisdom. Speak God's truth with God, who is Truth itself. Demonstrate the qualities of God, who is those Qualities. Practice God's actions every day of your life. Be within the justice of God and do what is just. Be within the compassionate eyes of God and then look at the world. Be in the state of God's peacefulness and try to give peace to the world. Be in the state of God's unity and then try to establish unity in the world.

When you exist in the state of God's actions, conduct, and behavior and speak with Him, that Power will speak with you. If you do not reach that state, then the words you speak will not be the truth. If you just keep the Bible or other scriptures on the outside, those scriptures will be merely books full of words. And that is all you will understand. But if you become a representative of God and speak with that Power, then that Power will speak with you. If you become a true man and a representative of God, then God will become your Master and you will understand the words which are His 'ilm, divine knowledge.

Until the day you find this state within yourself, you will only be studying the separations and differences that exist between races and religions. None of the lessons you learn in this world from books or scriptures, from poetry or other writings will ever bring you peace. You will never understand the meaning within them; you will only see the cover, the pages, and the letters. God's words are alive, shining as the resplendence within. If you cannot see that, you will never understand.

We must understand our story, God's story. We must know His Power, His vibration, His truth and peacefulness. Separations and differences are the faults within us that destroy our unity and peace. If we understand this, we will find peace in God's kingdom, in life, and in the family of mankind. Then we can truly understand the scriptures of Hinduism, Zoroastrianism, Christianity, Judaism, and Islām. They all contain the truth, but desire and the monkey mind have no truth. When we look through their eyes, with the thoughts of "our book" and "our sect," we see only differences. When we are under the influence of this chloroform, this alcohol, our wisdom is clouded and we see only differences. But when we free ourselves from this torpor and acquire God's qualities, wisdom, and actions, when we speak in that state as the representatives of God, then we will know the value of the Qur'ān, the Bible, and all the scriptures. Only then will we know the value of God and the value of man. How can we ever understand without achieving this state? Let us think about this.

When you dig a well, you must dig deep down until you reach a spring. Can the well ever be filled without reaching that deep source? If you depend upon the rain or some other outer source to fill the well, the water will simply evaporate or be absorbed by the earth. Then how can you wash yourself or quench your thirst? Only if you reach deep enough to find a spring will you come upon an undiminishing source of water. Similarly, if you only read the words of the scriptures, without digging deeper for their meaning, it is like digging a well without ever reaching the spring or like trying to fill it with rainwater. Neither will be sufficient. Only when you open that spring within and 'ilm, divine knowledge, flows from it will the water of God's qualities fill your heart. Only then can you receive His wealth. Only then will you find peace and tranquility. This *'ilm* and wisdom must arise from within you; the story of God and prayer must be understood from within. Then you will have all the water you need for yourself, and you will also have enough to share with others.

When a prospector searches for gold, he must sift the earth in order to extract this precious metal. He takes what is valuable and discards the rest. Similarly, wherever you search, whether it be in the east, west, north, or south, whether it be in Hinduism, Zoroastrianism, Christianity, Judaism, or Islām, you must search for and extract only that one valuable thing, the gold, the Treasure of Allāh, the Truth. As you search through all the scriptures, you must discard everything else, just as the prospectors discard the dirt and stones. God's wealth is all you need for your life and for the resplendence of your soul.

Until you understand this, you will know only disturbances in your life. Even if you rule the world, obtain titles and status, and acquire great treasures, gold, and land, you will never find peace. The only peace you can find is in God, in His qualities, His actions, His justice, His compassion, His patience, and His unity. Remember this.

Once you thought that everything you studied and learned was the truth. Then you progressed to the next step, and found that what you had learned was not the truth. In the future when you go still one step further and look back upon all that you presently hold to be true, you will see that it, too, is false. In this way, each time you advance to a new level, you will find that all you learned in the past was false. Finally, when you reach the state of God and the state of His wisdom, you will realize that all your thoughts were false, everything was false. God's wisdom is the real Truth, just as God's qualities are the real gold. Only He is the Truth.

When you understand this, you will ask His forgiveness for all the faults that you committed in the past. You will see clearly and absolutely that there is only one family, one prayer, and one God. You must think about this. This is the wisdom of truth, the valuable wisdom.

Therefore, find unity within yourself. Find peace within yourself. Find equality within yourself. Only when that spring opens within you and flows forth can you feed others and give them peace.

Children of wisdom, you must have love for God alone and faith in God alone. If you strengthen your *īmān* and open the spring of God's wisdom, then all the suffering of this birth, this mind, and this world will be washed away. All the opposition you face in this life, all the pain and suffering you may undergo at the time of death, and all the suffering you may have to face on Judgment Day will be cleansed by that water of God's grace. It will bring you to a state of death before death and make you a pure, resplendent light form. That faith will wash away the karma of your birth and transform you into a pure resplendence which no dirt can touch. You will become the resplendence within the Resplendence which is God. You will know the value and the beauty of God. You will shine as one who has destroyed the karma in all three worlds, and you will have freedom in all three worlds. You will realize that you came from Him, that you have grown within Him and become pure, and that He has accepted you. He will be a mystical Resplendence, and you will be a light form.

You must become one. Only if you pray to God with faith will peace and unity come to your life. And only then can you give peace to the world. Think about this. *Āmīn.*

PART TWO

HOLY WAR

CHAPTER FIVE

JIHĀD
The Holy War Within

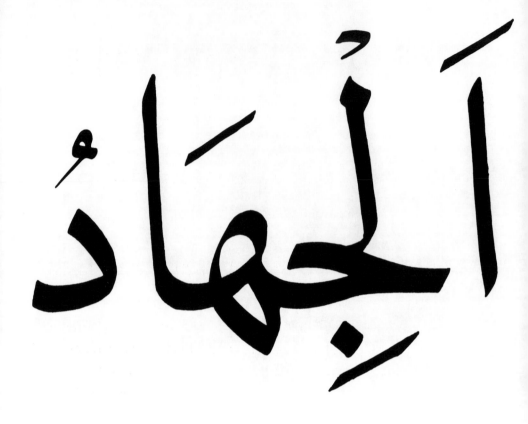

Al-Jihād
Holy war

The holy wars that the children of Adam ﷺ are waging today are not true holy wars. Taking other lives is not *jihād*. We will have to answer for that kind of *jihād* when we are questioned in the grave. That *jihād* is for the sake of men, for the sake of earth and wealth, for the sake of one's children, one's wife, and one's possessions. Selfish intentions are intermingled within that kind of *jihād*. True *jihād* is to praise God and cut away the inner satanic enemies.

CHAPTER FIVE

JIHĀD
The Holy War Within

I seek refuge in Allāh from the accursed satan.
In the name of Allāh, the Most Compassionate, the Most Merciful.

Allāhu *akbar*. Allāhu *akbar*. Lā *ilāha illAllāhu, Muhammadur-Rasūlullāh, sallallāhu 'alaihi wa sallam*: God is most great. God is most great. There is no God but Allāh, and Muhammad is the Messenger of Allāh, may the peace and blessings of Allāh be upon him.

My brothers and sisters in *Īmān*-Islām, we have affirmed the *ash-shahādah kalimah*: Ash-hadu al-lā ilāha illAllāhu, wahdahu lā sharīka lah; wa ash-hadu anna Muhammadan 'abduhu wa rasūluh.[1] We trust in God, we have faith in God, and we accept with *īmān* the revelations brought by the Rasūl ☺. This is justice and truth, and that truth is the silent witness of our life. It is the witness of *ākhirah*, the hereafter.

To accept and establish this state is *Īmān*-Islām. To recite the *kalimah* to Allāh with absolute faith, certitude, and determination, and to accept His representatives is *Īmān*-Islām. To

---

1. The Second *Kalimah*, the affirmation of faith. See Appendix.

pay obeisance to Him, to accept Him and worship Him alone, without the slightest doubt that Allāh is One, to become His 'abd, slave, and to bring His actions into ourselves by following and performing those actions is Īmān-Islām. This is Allāh's Qudrat, His Power, the wealth that emerges from the beauty of Islām.

My brothers and sisters, we have already talked a little about jihād, holy war. We have also spoken about the straight path and of the oneness of Allāh. This Unique, Almighty Power has no comparison; nothing is equal to Him, nothing can be likened to Him. That is why He is called the Incomparable One, and that is why we must accept Him.

The Qur'ān, the hadīth, and the kalimah are His signs. They provide explanations about His Power and His representatives. The entire Qur'ān is an explanation of the oneness of Allāh, and the kalimah verifies this oneness. The Qur'ān tells us that we are all the children of Adam ☺ and the slaves of Allāh, our Creator. The Qur'ān states this with certainty. Allāh is the One who gives according to the needs of each. He is the Unique One who will call us all back and question us later. He shows no differences among His creations; He creates, protects, and sustains us all. The Qur'ān states this with certainty, and we must understand this with our seven states of wisdom. We who are the children of Adam ☺ must fully accept Him within our hearts. We must bow down and prostrate before Him in sajdah and rukū'. That is the meaning of the kalimah and the meaning of Īmān-Islām. We must understand this.

My brethren, when God formed Adam ☺ out of earth, He placed the great trust of the Light of Nūr Muhammad[2] on

---

2. Nūr Muhammad (A) The beauty of the qualities and actions of the wilāyats, powers, of Allāh; the Light of Allāh's dhāt, essence, which shines within the resplendence of His truth.

Adam's ☺ forehead and decreed that man would know things that the angels and other beings could never know. Satan and those who joined with him were watching and listening. The leader of the jinns became filled with jealousy, pride, and vengeance, and these qualities changed him into satan. He began to speak against God, boasting to Adam ☺, "Allāh said that He created you to be most exalted, but I am more exalted than you. You are only made of earth. I am made of fire. If you bow down to me I will help you, but if you attempt to rise above me, I will do many evil things to you and make you suffer greatly."

Then that light on Adam's ☺ forehead looked closely at satan, causing an even greater fear, jealousy, and vengeance to arise within the leader of the jinns. Once again he defied Adam ☺. "You are created out of mere earth, and yet you dare to look at me like this! Until the very end, I will create sorrow and suffering for you, because you were given a higher place than I." Then he spat upon him. As soon as that spit landed on Adam ☺, satan's poisonous qualities entered him and spread through his entire body. Those qualities became the veils within the heart and the darkness of the mind.

Upon seeing what had happened, Allāh commanded the Angel Gabriel ☺ to pinch out the spot where satan's spit had fallen on Adam ☺, to clear that place of hell where those evil, envious qualities landed. The hollow that remained became the navel. Even though the spit was cleared away, some of the poison had already entered Adam ☺ and was passed on to mankind, causing endless trouble. Because of satan's actions, Allāh commanded that he and his followers be cast out of heaven. Then He elevated Adam ☺ to the high position decreed for him.

This is a very great matter. I am relating only a small part so that you may better understand the meaning of *jihād*, holy war.

Just as satan was thrown out of heaven because he opposed the Almighty, Unique One, we too must cast out all that is evil within us, everything that opposes God. Those evil qualities of jealousy and vengeance are the qualities that ruin us and take us on the path to hell. To wage *jihād* against these qualities is the most important *jihād*. This is the holy war that we must fight.

To help us do this Allāh sent down the *kalimah* and commanded, "Recite this *kalimah* and sever the enemy from within yourself. Who is the enemy? Satan. His evil qualities are the enemy to your body and to My unity and truth. Cut your connection to the evil one and dispel his qualities. Those satanic qualities are the fire of hell."

Therefore, with Allāh's qualities destroy the seven hells within you and through the *kalimah* embrace instead the purity of the oneness of Allāh. One who, with wisdom and a pure heart, accepts the oneness of Allāh completely, also accepts the *awwal*, first, *kalimah*. That is *tauhīd*, the affirmation of the unity of Allāh, and that is the first thing we have to do on the path of *Īmān*-Islām.

This explanation is very, very deep. This purity is very deep. The absolute faith, certitude, and determination called *īmān* is deep, and from it comes the wisdom which will help us to understand. We must accept the reality of the oneness and unity of Allāh. We must accept this without any doubt. And when we accept that Allāh is One, it means that we must also accept everyone, all of Adam's ☺ children as our brothers and sisters. We must think about this deeply, within our hearts.

My brothers, the holy wars that the children of Adam ☺ are waging today are not true holy wars. Taking other lives is not *jihād*. We will have to answer for that kind of *jihād* when we are questioned in the grave. That *jihād* is for the sake of men, for the sake of earth and wealth, for the sake of one's children, one's wife, and one's possessions. Selfish intentions are intermingled within that kind of *jihād*. True *jihād* is to praise God and cut away the inner satanic enemies. That is the one *jihād* that Allāh accepts. Among the seventy-three groups of mankind, there are only a few who understand and fight the true holy war against the enemy within themselves, the enemy who stands between them and Allāh, the enemy who does not accept Allāh and will not bow down and prostrate before Him. To wage war and cut our connection to this enemy who is leading us to hell is true *jihād*.

Brothers, once we realize who is the foremost enemy of this treasure of truth which we have accepted, then we can begin our holy war against that enemy. That is the *jihād* of *īmān,* of the *kalimah,* and of Islām.

When wisdom and clarity come to us, we will understand that the enemies of truth are within our own *qalbs*. There are four hundred trillion, ten thousand spiritual opponents within the body: satan and his qualities of backbiting, conceit, jealousy, envy, treachery, the separations of "I and you," "mine and yours," intoxicants, lust, theft, murder, falsehood, arrogance, karma, illusion, mantras and magics, and the desire for earth, woman, and gold. These are the enemies which separate us from Allāh, from truth, from *īmān* and worship, from good actions and good thoughts. These are the enemies which create divisions among the children of Adam ⊕ and prevent us from attaining a state of peace. We must wage war against these evil qualities within ourselves. We must not kill each other.

When a child has bad qualities, what does the mother do? She tries to teach him and help him to develop good qualities. Does she call him an evil child? No. If he steals the belongings of another because he wants to play with them, that is a bad quality no doubt, but the child is not evil. Does the mother strike down the child just because he has bad qualities? No. The mother explains things to the child and tries to expel the bad qualities and teach him good qualities. That is her duty, is it not?

Likewise, Allāh, who created us, does not strike down His creations for the evil they have committed. It would not make sense if He did that. They are all His children, the children of the Lord of all creation. As their Father and Mother, He helps them to dispel their evil ways and tries to bring them to the straight path. He seeks to make His children happy and good. That is the way God is. Just as God does not kill His children because they have evil qualities, it is not right for us to murder and cut down others. Instead, we must try to improve them by showing wisdom, love, compassion, and God's qualities, just as a mother teaches her playful child to change. That is our duty.

No good can come from cutting a person down. If the mother constantly shows unity and love to the child, then evil will leave. In the same way, we must remove these evil qualities from others, teach them good qualities, and lead them to the state where they can become the princes of God.

My brothers, if we act with love and unity, we can dispel our evil qualities and live as one family, as one race, as children bowing to one *Rabb*, Lord. Once we understand this truth, we will become good children. But as long as we do not understand and do not dispel the evil, then we are bad children.

Of course, when you cut these qualities, it might hurt. It might cause difficulty and suffering. When a child is cut, the pain makes him cry. He may scream and fight or maybe even bite you. He may shout, "I will kill you!" but you must embrace him with love and patiently explain things to him, always remembering that the qualities within the child are the enemy, not the child himself.

My brothers, we must realize that our fellow man is not the enemy, it is the qualities within him that are the enemy. Man has two forms, each with its own set of qualities. The war is between these two forms. One form is composed of the five elements and is ruled by the mind; it lives in the kingdom of illusion, creation, and hell. The other is a pure form made of Allāh's Light, of His Resplendence and Purity; it lives in the kingdom of heaven, in the world of pure souls. When man dwells within this good form, he speaks and acts in good ways. When he moves into the form of the elements, he speaks and acts in evil ways. One body exists within him in a formless state; the other exists outside as his form and shadow. These two bodies have opposite qualities and duties.

There are also two sections in the heart: one is the *qalb,* the inner heart, and the other is the mind. The mind is connected to the fifteen worlds, which are ruled by the five elements of earth, fire, water, air, and ether. We can see how these five elements are mixed together in the earth and in the sky. They are mingled within the body in the same way.

These fifteen worlds are connected to creation and to all forms. Seven of the worlds are above, seven are below, and the fifteenth world, which is in the center, is the mind. It is there, in the world ruled by the mind, that *jihād* must be waged. The mind and the energies of the elements roam up and down throughout the fifteen worlds. These energies, *shaktis,* manifest as the four hundred trillion, ten thousand spiritual miracles and create differences and divisions among men. We have to fight against all these energies in all fifteen worlds. This is the major battle. Once we complete this war, then we are ready to begin our work within the *qalb,* the inner heart.

The *qalb* is the kingdom of Allāh. The *sirr,* secret, of the eighteen thousand universes and the secret of this world are contained within that heart. Allāh's messengers, His representatives, the angels, prophets, saints, the resplendently pure souls, and His Light within the soul are all to be found in a point, a mere *nuqtah,* within the *qalb.* His entire kingdom is contained within an atom within the *qalb.* That is His *dhāt,* essence. That is the kingdom of truth and purity, the kingdom of heaven. The eighteen thousand universes are within that kingdom of divine wisdom, *gnānam.* That is the kingdom of light and *'ilm,* divine knowledge, the kingdom of justice and truth.

Allāh is the Ruler of all these universes. His infinite Power, *Qudrat,* His three thousand gracious qualities, His ninety-nine *wilāyats,* attributes, His compassion, peace, unity, and equality are all found within these universes. That is the *qalb,* His kingdom of *īmān* and justice, where one can find peace. Until we reach that kingdom, we have to wage a holy war within ourselves.

In order to show us how to cut away this enemy that exists within us and to teach us how to establish the connection with Him, Allāh sent down 124,000 prophets, twenty-five of whom are described thoroughly in the Qur'ān. These prophets came to teach us how to wage holy war against the inner enemy. This battle within should be fought with *īmān,* with the *kalimah,* and with the Qur'ān. No blood is shed in this war. Holding the sword of wisdom, faith, *īmān,* and justice, we must cut away the evil forces that keep charging at us in different forms. This is the inner *jihād.*

My brothers in *Īmān*-Islām, we must cut away all of those qualities which oppose Allāh. There are no other enemies. Allāh has no enemies. If anyone were to oppose Allāh, the All-Powerful, Unique One, he could never be victorious. You cannot raise or lower Allāh. He does not accept praise or blame.

Praising Allāh and then destroying others is not *jihād.* Some groups wage war against the children of Adam ⊕ and call it *jihād,* but for man to raise his sword against man, for man to kill man, is not *jihād.* There is no point in that. There can be no benefit from killing a man in the name of God. Allāh has no thought of killing other lives or going to war. Why would Allāh have sent His prophets if He had such thoughts? It was not to harm men that the Rasūl ⊕ and the other prophets came. The Rasūl ⊕ was sent down as the wisdom that could show man how to cut his evil qualities within.

It is the qualities of satan within us that are our enemies, not other men. Once we have completely severed these, there will be no more enmity among human beings. All will live as brothers and sisters. That is true Islām, the unity of Allāh, the oneness of Allāh. That is *tauhīd.* Once we accept this, Allāh accepts us. Once we fight and conquer these enemies of our *īmān,* these enemies of our prayers, we will find peace within ourselves. Once we have found peace within, we will find peace everywhere. This world will be heaven, and we will have a direct connection to Allāh, just as Adam ⊕ had that original connection. Then we will understand the connection between ourselves and all the children of Adam ⊕.

Every child must know this and fight the enemy within. We must fight the battle of *halāl* against *harām,* the battle between that which is permissible under God's law and that which is forbidden. If we do not do this, then the qualities of evil, *sharr,* will kill that which is good, *khair,* and the truth will be destroyed. But if we can complete this huge battle, we will receive Allāh's *rahmah,* His grace, and that will enable us to know His eighteen thousand universes. If we can conquer the world of the mind, we will see the kingdom of the soul, His kingdom.

May every one of us think about this and wage our own holy

war. Only when we complete the battle and progress beyond will we realize that we are all children of Adam ☺, that we are all one race, that there is only one prayer, and that there is only One who is worthy of worship, one God, one Lord, one Rahmān, one Rahīm. He is the Merciful One. He creates and sustains all lives, He does not cut them down. Once we realize this, there will be no more fighting, no more spilling of blood, no more murder.

We will never attain peace and equality within our *qalbs* until we finish this war and conquer the armies that arise from the thoughts and differences within ourselves, until we attack these enemies with the faith, certitude, and determination of *īmān*, and with *sabūr*, inner patience, *shukūr*, contentment, *tawakkul*, trust in God, and *al-hamdu lillāh*, all praise is to God. With *'ilm*, divine knowledge, with justice and conscience, we must fight and win this inner *jihād*.

As-salāmu 'alaikum. May the peace of God be with you. Allāh is sufficient for all. *Āmīn.*

CHAPTER SIX

THE
WEAPONS
OF ISLĀM

As-Sabūr Ash-Shukūr

Inner patience   Contentment

At-Tawakkul

Trust in God

Al-hamdu lillāh

Praise of God

    Once we understand what the true weapons of Islām are, we will never take a life, we will not murder, and we will not see anyone as separate from ourselves. We will not even conceive of any enmity....We will realize that each and every brother must act in accordance with Allāh's actions and with the same *sabūr, shukūr, tawakkul,* and *al-hamdu lillāh* shown by the Rasūlullāh ⊕.

CHAPTER SIX

THE WEAPONS OF ISLĀM

—·◈· ◇✦◇ ·◈·—

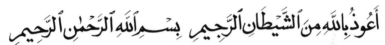

I seek refuge in Allāh from the accursed satan.
In the name of Allāh, the Most Compassionate, the Most Merciful.

As-salāmu ʻalaikum. May the peace of God be upon all my brothers and sisters in *Īmān*-Islām. May all responsibility be offered to Allāhu taʻālā, the Most Exalted One, the Unfathomable Ruler of grace who is incomparable love. *Āmīn*. You alone are responsible for the Day of Questioning, *Qiyāmah*, and the Day of Judgment, for the beginning of life and the time of death, for life in this world and the next. You confer that *rahmah*, grace, ask the questions, and give the judgment. You are the *Rahmatul-ʻālamīn*, the Mercy and Compassion for all the universes. *Āmīn. Āmīn.*

Yā Allāh, You are the Light and the Plenitude of *dīn,*[1] the *rahmah* of *dīn*, the grace of perfect purity. May You be the protector of the people of *dīn*. May You make *dīn* the complete, never-ending wealth of grace in the *qalbs* of those who are on the path known as the light of *īmān*, of faith, certitude, and determination. May You show them the way and give them Your grace. *Āmīn.*

---

1. *dīn* (A) The light of perfect purity; the resplendence of *īmān*, absolute faith. Literally, faith, belief, religion.

Yā Allāh, may You help all those who have received the *rahmah* of Islām and have made that *rahmah* their never-ending wealth. May they never lose their way on the path of *dīn*. May You reveal the true path to them, and may they proceed on that path to *firdaus,* Your heavenly paradise. *Āmīn.* May You grant those of purity, *dīn,* the undiminishing wealth of Your grace. *Āmīn.*

As-salāmu 'alaikum wa rahmatullāhi wa barakātuhu. May the peace, the beneficence, and the blessings of God be upon you. I give my *salāms,* greetings of peace, to all of my very precious brothers, my exalted brothers in Islām who are one through the light of the Qur'ān and who have been given the wealth of *īmān,* my brothers who are great and wise in Islām, who have received the wealth of unending life, the *hayāh* of *īmān,* the eternal life of absolute faith. To all my eight hundred million brothers in Islām I give my humble *salāms.*

Allāh sent 124,000 prophets to explain His laws and codes of behavior. Of these 124,000, He chose twenty-five and sent them bearing His sound and His revelations, *wahys.* To reveal His truth and strengthen our *īmān,* Allāh gave these messengers the holy words of grace for all three worlds. He sent them so that each heart would open and develop *īmān.* Every prophet told us to love Allāh, to accept Him with determined faith, and to worship and pray to Him without any racial or religious prejudice.

It was to bring this message that Allāhu ta'ālā, God, the Most Exalted, sent so many prophets through His holy grace. Then He made His resonance into the teachings of the Holy Qur'ān, and sent that to the Final Prophet, Muhammad Mustāfār-Rasūl ☻, the Chosen Messenger. Through the Angel Gabriel ☻, Allāh revealed to Muhammad ☻ His words, His actions, His conduct, His goodness, and His *wilāyats.* We must reflect deeply upon every explanation contained within this Holy Qur'ān, which exists in the three realms of *awwal, dunyā,* and *ākhirah,* the beginning, this world, and the hereafter.

We who are the community of Islām must remember that ultimately everything was given to Islām. What was given? Allāhu ta'ālā gave *salāh,* prayer, to Islām as a weapon in this world and the next. He ordained that the fifty times of prayer, *waqts,* be made into five. With *sabūr,* inner patience, *shukūr,* contentment, *tawakkul,* trust in God, and *al-hamdu lillāh,* all praise is to God, we must use this weapon of prayer to fight the inner war and eliminate the enmity and hatred within ourselves. We must dispel our *nafs,* base desires, our prejudices, our religious and racial differences, the countless demons and ghosts of arrogance, and the karma and illusion within our bodies. Pride, jealousy, the sense of separation between men, and all other evils must be fought with this weapon which the Rasūlullāh ☉ brought and offered as the final teaching to those who are in *dīn,* the path of perfect purity.

In addition to the five times prayer, Allāhu ta'ālā ordained the five *furūd,* obligatory duties, for the Muslim community. The first *fard,* obligatory duty, is to accept the oneness of Allāh with certitude. All those in Islām who have that perfect *īmān* must wholeheartedly accept the *kalimah,* which declares that nothing exists but Allāhu ta'ālā. The second *fard* is to worship Allāh alone, to worship Him as the *Rabb,* the Lord, without any equal and without any partner. It is to have *īmān,* absolute trust, certitude, and faith in Him alone. The third *fard* is to share the grace of Allāh, His *rahmah,* with all your brothers, to comfort and care for them as you would care for yourself. At the very least you must give charity before *jum'ah* prayers, the congregational prayers on Friday. You must understand that whatever wealth you have does not belong to you, it belongs to Allāh and must be shared with all your brothers. This is *zakāh,* charity.

But for those who did not observe the third *fard* correctly, Allāh ordained the fourth duty of fasting, *saum,* so that they might come to a realization of themselves. Allāh told them to undertake a compulsory fast of thirty days in succession and ten more days of *sunnah,* optional, fast as well. The purpose of fasting is to become aware of your own hunger, your own condition, and your own suffering. That is true fasting. If you understand that, you will share your food and wealth with your brothers.

But because this duty was not observed correctly either, Allāh ordained the fifth *fard* of *hajj.* True *hajj,* pilgrimage, is to enter the state of dying before death. For the poor, the *miskīns* who cannot afford a pilgrimage to Mecca, *hajj* means going each Friday to the *jum'ah* prayers in their own town or city. For the rich, *hajj* is a pilgrimage to Mecca and Medina. Before going on this journey the pilgrim must give away everything he possesses. The *mahr,* dowry, of his wife must be returned and his wealth distributed among his relatives. The pilgrims must wear a white shroud and go in a state resembling a corpse, a *mayyit.*

We who are in Islām must understand and act in accordance with these *furūd.* These too are weapons of Islām. Along with the five-times prayer they help us to overcome hell, satan, and evil qualities. These are truly great weapons, and with them we must fight the huge battle in our hearts. That is where we must overcome everything that covers the truth, all that is *kufr,* unbelieving. We must overcome our *kufr* minds, our *kufr* thoughts, our *kufr qalbs, kufr* acts, the *kufr* darkness, the *kufr* eating of *harām* food, *kufr* pride, jealousy, vengeance, treachery, trickery, and the magic of illusion and unreality. Allāhu ta'ālā sent these weapons to us through the Rasūl ☻ so that we would be able to overcome all these evils.

My precious brothers in the community of Islām, who have

been granted *īmān* and have received the *barakah* of *dīn,* the blessing of perfect purity, in all three worlds, all my brothers in *dīn*—these are the weapons that were given to the Rasūlullāh ☻, and they are also our weapons. To put them to use is Islam. These are the weapons for those who are of the faith called *dīn,* which is known as Islam.

Each person in Islam must understand where this real war must be fought, where the real battlefield exists. Each must understand what it is that is dividing and destroying Islam, what it is that is denying Allāh and breaking up His kingdom. Each must understand what jealousy is, what pride is, and what the selfishness that says, "Mine!" is. To cut away all these things, Allāh sent us the five times of prayer, the five *furūd,* and the strength of *sabūr, shukūr, tawakkul,* and *al-hamdu lillāh.* This is the final message given to the Rasūl ☻, and we who are in the community of Islam must understand these teachings.

My brothers, to further our understanding we must reflect upon the life of the Prophet ☻. When Abū Jahl, Ikrimah, Habīb ibn Mālik,[2] and others who opposed the Rasūlullāh ☻ chased him out of Mecca, they caused him great suffering. They even tried to kill him. Islam must realize that they did this because they kept their gods of the past within themselves—their mantras, their magics, their family gods, their idols, and their satans,

---

2. Abū Jahl: One of the foremost adversaries of Muhammad ☻. His real name was 'Amr ibn Hishām but the Muslims nicknamed him Abū Jahl, or the "Father of Ignorance."

   Ikrimah: The son of Abū Jahl. For many years, along with his father, he was a determined opponent of Muhammad ☻. However he later embraced Islam and became a companion of the Prophet ☻.

   Habīb ibn Mālik: A prince of the major Arabian tribes who was asked by Abū Jahl to question Muhammad ☻ in the hope of proving him a false prophet. According to some narratives, Muhammad ☻ performed several miracles, including the splitting of the moon (referred to in the 54th chapter of the Qur'ān), thus convincing Habīb and converting him to Islam.

some of which could talk. In the darkness of their worship, they made offerings and sacrifices to these idols of darkness. They worshipped forty-eight thousand idols, three hundred and sixty of which could be seen, large and small, housed in the Ka'bah.

At that time, the fire of satan, the pride of satan, and the qualities of satan were alive, manifesting as the anger of man. So God sent the Light, the *rahmah* of Muhammad ☻, to fight that darkness. When God sent Muhammad ☻ as the Light, the darkness became his enemy, chasing him and his companions, *as-hāb*, from Mecca to Medina. But the *as-hāb* had the *salāh*, and they had *sabūr, shukūr, tawakkul,* and *al-hamdu lillāh.* Allāh said to them, "These are the weapons which will cut through the darkness and overcome enmity. They will overcome the separations, egoism, and prejudices present in the minds that are *kufr*, that reject faith. These weapons are a radiant light which will sever the darkness and prove that Allāh alone exists."

Allāh gave these weapons to the Rasūl ☻, telling him, "*Yā* Muhammad, say, *'Lā ilāha illAllāh.* There is no God but Allāh. There is no one worthy of worship other than Allāhu ta'ālā.' Teach the people this *kalimah.* That is why I sent it to you. Explain it to them, and tell them to accept Me.

"Explain to them that *awwal, dunyā,* and *ākhirah,* the time of creation, this world, and the hereafter, are My kingdom. I am the Ruler, I am the Judge, I alone provide the food for the living and the dead, and I am the One who will ask the questions on Judgment Day. I am the One who judges. Teach this to the people."

So that Allāh's commandments would be accepted, Muhammad ☻ sent these words to every nation. He told them, "Allāhu ta'ālā is the Ruler of grace, the One of *rahmah.* He has no children, no relations, no comparison, no equal. He is the Eternal

One, the Omnipresent, Eternal Ruler, who guides us along the true path."

Muhammad ☺ spread these words throughout the land, by way of his messengers. Some people accepted Allāh, but others did not. The kingdoms where Allāh was not accepted were destroyed by fire, by water, by hurricane, by battle, and by the arrogance and pride of the people. Destruction came and lands were covered by oceans, cities became jungles, and villages became cemeteries. But every place that accepted Allāh was under His safekeeping, and became the kingdom of God, the kingdom of *īmān*.

Abū Jahl and his followers were among those who did not accept Allāh's message, and it was because of them that the battles of Badr and Uhud[3] were fought and many people were killed. But those battles were not fought to conquer other nations. They were fought to conquer the qualities of satan that refused to accept Allāh. They were battles between the truth of Allāh and falsehood. They were fought so that people could pray, worship, and accept His judgment, and so that justice would prevail.

It would be very good if every *qalb* of the eight hundred million people of Islām understood this. The Rasūlullāh ☺ did not fight to usurp land or gold or to capture women. The commandments of Allāh tell us not to try to rule the world, but instead to rule the *qalb* of *insān,* the inner heart of a human being, the place known as the *'arshul-mu'min,* the throne of the true believer, His

---

3. The battle of Badr was fought between the followers of Muhammad ☺ and those among the Quraish who rejected the belief in Allāh and Muhammad ☺. Many of Islām's principal opponents were killed, including Abū Jahl. The victory of Badr established the ability of the Muslims to defend themselves.

The battle of Uhud was also between the followers of Muhammad ☺ and the Quraish. The outcome of the battle was mixed, the Muslims being outflanked by Khālid ibnul-Walīd, a great warrior among the Quraish who later embraced Islām. The Quraish, however, did not pursue their advantage and were forced to retreat by the regrouped Muslims.

kingdom. Allāh is the only One who can rule that kingdom. He rules each *qalb* with the wealth of the *rahmatul-'ālamīn,* with His justice, His *sabūr,* patience, and His *wilāyats,* attributes. Anyone who can rule in this manner is a true ruler. Whether he is a political leader, an *imām* who leads the prayers, or an *'ālim,* a learned teacher, the one who can rule the hearts of the people is the exalted *mu'min,* the *insān kāmil,* a God-realized being.

My brothers, we must use *sabūr,* inner patience, to acquire those qualities which can rule the heart. That is the greatest kingdom of all, and to govern there is the most exalted rulership. Those who do not govern the people's hearts but instead rule over the earth, really govern in hell. Such things belong to hell, to the *la'natul-jahannam,* the curse of hell. Pride is hell, and the attractions of earth, gold, woman, and possessions are advertisements that lure us to the seven hells. To overcome those hells we must begin to govern the heart with good qualities, with prayer, and with *'ibādah,* worship. Those who are in Islām must realize this.

The wars during the time of the Rasūlullāh ☺ were fought so that truth would be accepted, but the wars we are engaged in today are being fought for the sake of conquering nations, capturing countries, and killing and vanquishing others. This is not the kind of war that true Islām wages. Each of us must remember this. We must realize that it is not right for us to display such hostility. *Sabūr,* inner patience, and compassion are appropriate for us. We must realize that it is not right for us to harbor hatred. *Shukūr,* contentment, is appropriate for us at all times, in all circumstances. We must realize that it is not right for us to be angry, because anger belongs to satan. Only *tawakkulun 'alAllāh,* absolute trust in God, is appropriate for Islām. We must give all praise to Allāh for the food that we eat during each *waqt.* We must say, "*Al-hamdu lillāh,*" and praise God for everything we receive in our lives, whether it be a great feast or a glass of water, immense wealth or dire poverty. To praise Allāh at each moment, no matter what happens, is Islām.

Enmity cannot be overcome with enmity. Each of you must realize that in true Islām enmity does not exist. If you see someone else as your enemy, it is your own reflection that you are seeing. Hostility cannot be overcome by hostility; to overcome it, you must first rid yourself of your own hostility and then have *sabūr*. Vengeance cannot be defeated by vengeance; if you want to defeat it, you must first overcome your own vengeance and then practice love and compassion. You must do this with *sabūr, shukūr, tawakkul,* and *al-hamdu lillāh.* Jealousy cannot be overcome by jealousy. It was because of satan's jealousy that he ruined Adam ⊕. If you let that quality grow within yourself, you can never subdue it in others. However, if you can overcome your own jealousy with compassion, *sabūr,* and *shukūr,* then you can help others to overcome theirs.

Hatred cannot be overcome by hatred, nor anger by anger. Anger is fire, and God created the jinns and their leader, satan, out of that fire. Because of his hatred and anger, satan was hurled from heaven into this world of hell. Anyone who has that anger in him is a satan. If we are angry, we will see anger in others, but if we overcome satan's anger in ourselves, we will not see it in anyone else.

It is our own satanic qualities that must be overcome with *sabūr, shukūr, tawakkul,* and *al-hamdu lillāh.* However, if instead we nourish these evil qualities, then Allāh will throw us away from Himself. Just as He cast off satan, He will throw us out of heaven into hell.

In this world there are four hundred trillion, ten thousand spiritual energies given shape by satan's magic, his trickery, and his treachery. They are found in the earth, air, fire, water, and ether of the body. If we can overcome these evil energies within ourselves, then we can see heaven there. And if heaven exists within us, we can embrace everyone equally. We can have compassion for everyone and be loving, tolerant, peaceful, and patient to everyone. We can be filled with *shukūr, tawakkul,* and *al-hamdu lillāh* and receive Allāh's *rahmah,* His grace. This must be realized within the *qalb* of everyone in Islām.

My brothers, once we understand what the true weapons of Islām are, we will never take a life, we will not murder, and we will not see any brother as separate from ourselves. We will not even conceive of any enmity. Allāhu ta'ālā revealed and explained this state to His Rasūl ☽, and we who are Islām must understand. When we do, we will know Allāh and His state as revealed in the ninety-nine *wilāyats,* attributes, of the *asmā'ul-husnā.* We will realize that each and every brother must act in accordance with Allāh's actions and with the same *sabūr, shukūr, tawakkul,* and *al-hamdu lillāh* shown by the Rasūlullāh ☽. Patience and the three thousand beautiful qualities of Allāh are the *rahmatul-'ālamīn,* the mercy and compassion for all the universes, and the wealth of Islām. If we have this, we will not feel hatred or enmity for anyone or for any nation.

Allāhu ta'ālā gave this *dunyā,* world, to everyone. In a *hadīth qudsī,* a direct revelation to the Prophet ☽, Allāh said, "*Firdaus,* the eighth heaven, is My nation, and everyone who comes here belongs to one family. I dispense judgment, and there are no separations here, no differences of color, religion, race, language, or scripture. There is only one place for everyone who accepts Me. In *firdaus,* you are all the children of Adam, each of you will have a place in accordance with the way you search for Me. I will give you your appropriate rewards."

All who are great and wise in the community of Islām—the rulers and those who serve the rulers, the *'ulamā'*, teachers, the *auliyā'*, saints, and the *qutbs*, the great holy men of divine wisdom—must know that Allāhu ta'ālā has given to each of His creations the appropriate place at the appropriate time. He gave the snake its hole and the ant its anthill. He made places for the reptiles and for the birds. He gave the jinns and fairies places to live, He gave the *malaks*, angels, and *malā'ikah*, archangels, places, and He even gave a place to satan and to evil. He made room for both light and darkness, for *halāl* and *harām*, that which is permissible according to God's law and that which is forbidden. He made room for everyone. He made separate places for men and beasts so that each would have his own particular dwelling. Allāhu ta'ālā provided a place for all the children of Adam ☺, for all the children of every religion, race, and language. In the same way, Allāh provided a place for each prophet.

Islām does not usurp that which was given to another by God; it neither destroys nor takes anyone else's place. There is no room in Islām for hurting others, taking their possessions or their homes. Islām sees its neighbors as brothers, not as different or separate. It does not kill others. It shows them love, compassion, and patience, and gives them the wealth of *īmān*, faith, *sabūr*, inner patience, *shukūr*, contentment, and *tawakkul*, trust in God. True Islām brings only peace; it contains no enmity whatsoever. We who are in Islām must realize this and know that Allāhu ta'ālā has given to every creation a place, a country, a spouse, a treasure, or a kingdom. We must be content and say, "*Tawakkulun 'alAl-lāh*, Allāh is responsible for everything. *Al-hamdu lillāh*, all praise is due to Him alone."

It is our responsibility to accept Allāh and the teachings of the Rasūl ☺. But over the last hundred years some people of Islām and of other religions have changed. Faith has decreased to the point where many say that God does not exist. The darkness and torpor of desire for earth, woman, and gold have entered our hearts and changed us. We must dispel this darkness from our *qalbs*, inner hearts. Jealousy, vengeance, the qualities of satan, anger, sin, and pride have come into us. The Rasūlullāh ☺ chased all these away from us before, but now they have returned.

So we must strengthen our *īmān*, and using the weapons of the five-times prayer and of *sabūr, shukūr, tawakkul*, and *al-hamdu lillāh*, we must once again chase away those evil qualities from our hearts. Our job is not to chase others from their homes, or wage war against others, or kill them, or cause them pain, because they too are the children of Adam ☺. We who are in Islām must never hurt anyone. We have to understand this. The *hadīth*, the words of the Rasūlullāh ☺, and the explanations of the Qur'ān tell us very clearly the way we must live. I humbly plead with you to do this. True Islām must be reestablished and again receive the *daulah*, the wealth, of prayer. You and I, all of us, must live entirely in a state of *sabūr, shukūr, tawakkul*, and *al-hamdu lillāh*.

Over fourteen hundred years ago Allāh sent the *dīn*, the purity of Islām, to the Prophet Muhammad Mustāfā, the Chosen Messenger ☺. There is a *hadīth*, a traditional story, about this. Some of the *as-hāb*, companions of the Rasūl ☺, asked how long *dīn* would last in the world. And the Rasūl ☺ of Allāhu ta'ālā said, "The *dīn* will be protected for fourteen hundred years. During that time it will be safe, but afterwards, *tawakkulun 'alAllāh*, He alone knows what will happen to Islām."

That time is *now*. Those fourteen hundred years have passed. Today is the time the Rasūlullāh ☺ was referring to. *Tawakkulun 'alAllāh*, God alone knows the fate of Islām. If we consider what is happening in Islām today, we will be able to understand why this was said. Faith in Allāh and focus on Allāh have decreased tremendously. Islām no longer seems to understand the difference between *halāl* and *harām,* what is permissible according to God's law and what is forbidden, between *sharr* and *khair,* good and evil, right and wrong, or between truth and falsehood. Islamic people have turned to war and fighting. They no longer seem to fear the Day of Questioning, *Qiyāmah,* or even the Day of Judgment. Wherever we look, we see Islamic nations allying themselves with those who have no faith in God, with those who deny God. They have turned to tigers and to the enemies of Allāh for help.

We who are in Islām must remember that Allāh is our only helper every second, every minute, every hour, every *waqt,* time of prayer. Allāh is our Ruler, the Ruler of grace, the One who is Love, the Compassionate One, the One who calls us back to Him, the One who questions us, and the One who judges us. His *rahmah,* grace, exists in all lives, concealed within a tiny piece of flesh within the inner heart, the *qalb.* Just as the flesh of the tongue knows taste, just as the flesh of the nose perceives smell and the flesh of the ear hears sound and the flesh of the eye perceives light—like that, there is a tiny piece of flesh in the heart which worships Allāh, looks at Him, hears Him, and prays to Him. This is the *'arshul-mu'min,* the throne of the true believer. This is where Allāh dwells. This is His *dahūt,* the throne within the *qalb,* from which He rules and dispenses justice. It is the seat of judgment in this world and the next. Without our awareness, that piece of flesh, that light, that *rahmah,* discerns the difference between good and evil. In the same way that our senses perceive physical things, it discerns good and evil in whatever the eyes see, the nose smells, the ears hear, and the tongue tastes. It discerns the good and evil in our thoughts and intentions. This tiny piece of flesh is hidden within the body of the elements, but it cannot be destroyed by earth, fire, air, or water. It is this which will rise on the Day of *Qiyāmah,* the Day of Questioning.

To make it possible to discover this secret, Allāhu ta'ālā placed the radiance of *Nūr Muhammad* in the *'arsh,* God's throne on the crown of the head, as the resplendent wisdom of man. Each heart has a scale, a *mīzān,* which uses wisdom to weigh good and evil, to judge right and wrong. We must attach the trays of *"lā ilāha:* there is nothing other than You, O God, and *illAllāhu:* Only You are God," to the scale of *īmān* and put everything we collect in our lives on either the left or the right tray. Instead of nourishing hostility or evil, we should avoid them. We should place them on the left side of the scale and read the gauge, the indicator of wisdom, so that we can eliminate the evil and gather up the good.

This is judgment, and Islām must understand this judgment. If we understand right and wrong and *khair* and *sharr,* good and evil, in this world, if we understand them with our *īmān,* the *kalimah,* and the qualities of Allāh, we will push away every bad thing and do only what is right. We will rid ourselves of all that is *sharr,* evil. Then we can put truth in our treasury, in the *daulah,* wealth, of Allāh where complete *tawakkulun 'alAllāh* and *al-hamdu lillāh* exist. Each *qalb* must think about this.

Īmān-Islām must give the treasures of satan to satan and the treasures of Allāh to Allāh. With trust and surrender to God, with *tawakkulun 'alAllāh,* Islām must gather up the treasures of truth. Today in Islām, we have forgotten Allāh. We have tried to rule the *dunyā,* the world, forfeiting the *rahmah* of Allāh and instead accepting the wealth of the *dunyā.* We have begun to consider earth, woman, and gold as our wealth, even though they can all be destroyed in a second by an earthquake, a hurricane, or a storm.

When Abraham ☺ was put into a fiery pit, he sought the help of Allāh alone. He would not ask for anyone else's help. If those of us who have *īmān* also seek only His help, that *rahmah* will be endless. But if we seek the world and its material treasures, all that will change and leave us one day. The land will be covered by oceans, cities will be turned into forests, and villages will become cemeteries. Worldly wealth changes that way and is finally destroyed.

Everyone in Islām who has *īmān,* absolute faith, certitude, and determination, must know this and accept it. Instead of trying to capture the wealth of the world, we must earn the wealth of *īmān.* The treasures in our lives must be *sabūr,* inner patience, *shukūr,* contentment, *tawakkul,* trust in God, and *al-hamdu lil-lāh,* all praise is to God; as well as *salāh,* prayer, *'ibādah,* worship, *dhikr,* remembrance of God, and *fikr,* contemplation on God. We must have Allāh's three thousand gracious, beautiful qualities and His ninety-nine *wilāyats,* attributes. We must use each action which Allāh revealed to us in His *wilāyats.* If we do, Islām will never be destroyed, it will never be degraded, and it will never be in danger. We must realize this and fill ourselves with *sabūr* so that we can overcome any enmity within us.

Everyone filled with the light of *īmān* must reflect on this. True Islām means cutting away all hostility within ourselves, embracing everyone in brotherhood, uniting congregation with congregation. We must remember that all the children of Adam ☺ will become one congregation on the Day of *Qiyāmah,* the Day of Questioning, in heaven, in paradise, in the kingdom of Allāh. Everyone in Islām must remember this.

If we all accepted and understood this, we would not fight. We would know that our only enemies are those who do not accept Allāh, those who deny Allāh and see Him as their enemy. Islām is not war, it is not murder, it is not battles. This is not what we must engage in. Peace is Islām, *sabūr,* inner patience, is Islām, *shukūr,* contentment, is Islām, *tawakkul,* trust in God, is Islām, *al-hamdu lillāh,* all praise is to God, is Islām. Love is Islām. This is the umbrella, the canopy of goodness which Allāhu ta'ālā sent to Muhammad Mustāfar-Rasūl, the Chosen Messenger ☺. He received it from Allāh and gave it to us. If we fill our *qalbs,* inner hearts, with this love, then no hatred, no battle, no bloodshed will ever befall us. If we understand this, we will see peace in the whole world. Radiance, light, and truth will illuminate our lives and our *qalbs.*

The Qur'ān has protected those with *īmān* since the Rasūl ☺ first came. Not one drop of blood of the prophets or of the *mu'mins,* who are the perfect followers of the Rasūl ☺, or of those who are in *Īmān-*Islām may be spilled on this earth. The earth will not drink the blood of those who have accepted *īmān* fully and have the light of perfect purity. If the blood of those lights of Allāh should ever be shed, then that land where that crime occurred will be completely destroyed.

My brothers, we have not come here to shed blood. Those with *īmān* have not come to shed blood. We have come to make peace between the world and heaven, the world and eternity. We have come here to live in peace, with patience. We have come to implant that *rahmah* and light of *īmān* in each heart and open the path to *firdaus,* the eighth heaven. With the qualities of the Rasūl ☺ and the qualities and actions of the ninety-nine *wilāyats,* attributes, of Allāh as examples, we must offer peace and comfort to everyone and try to take each one of our brothers along the straight, true path.

Our true state is peace; our true state is *sabūr, shukūr, tawak-kul,* and *al-hamdu lillāh.* This is the *rahmah* of Islām, the wealth of our life. Once we understand this grace and behave as those in Islām should, all the creatures of land and sea, the jinns and fairies, each and every one of Allāh's creations will prostrate before that light and worship that beauty of Islām. If we trust in God completely and surrender all responsibility to Him, everything will subordinate itself to Islām and prostrate to that purity. Except for satan, there is no opposition to true Islām. All others will prostrate themselves. This is shown with perfect clarity and perfect resplendence in the Qur'ān, which came to us as Allāh's resonance and was explained to us by the Rasūl ☺. Each one of us with *īmān* must realize this true state and then help others to change.

People need water to survive; even if there is no food to eat, they must at least have water. The *rahmah* of Allāh is the water of *Īmān*-Islām. When you see someone starving for that water of *rahmah,* you must give him some, revive him, take him away from the sufferings of the world, nurture his life, change his state, and help him to follow God's laws. This is *īmān.*

My brothers, you must quench the thirst of all lives with that *rahmah* and let them rest. You must heal the sufferings of the world. This is the wealth, the *rahmatul-'ālamīn,* the mercy and compassion of all the universes that has been given to mankind, and we who have accepted *īmān* must strive to offer it to all. We should not carry a sword in our hands; we should hold *sabūr* in our hearts. We should not arm ourselves with guns; we should be armed with *shukūr.* We should not put our trust in battles; we should have the trust of *tawakkulun 'alAllāh.* We should not cling to the world; we should cling to *al-hamdu lillāh,* the praise of God. These are the true weapons of Islām.

My brothers in Islām, all the leaders of the world, all the learned, exalted people of wisdom who have faith in the Qur'ān, all who believe in Allāh and in the Rasūl ☺, all who have the right to the dignity of Islām—you must bring peace to the world.

Chase away the arrogance, darkness, and demons that lurk in the heart. With the weapons of love, *sabūr*, and *shukūr*, conquer those hearts and unite them under the umbrella of Islām, under the flag of *Īmān*-Islām, under the light of the Rasūl ☺. Those hearts will all melt and prostrate to that love. The Rasūl ☺ had no warlike qualities. He had only the qualities of *sabūr*, *shukūr*, *tawakkul*, and *al-hamdu lillāh*. If those qualities are reestablished in each *qalb*, if they flourish and grow in each heart, then Islām will become a vast, protective canopy for the world.

If everyone in the community of Islām understood this and tried to establish peace, tolerance, and patience, that alone would bring peace to the world. The weapons of peace and tranquility will grant us victory no matter what enmity, what hostility, threatens us. We must realize this, my brothers in Islām. If we do, we will triumph in all three worlds, in *awwal*, *dunyā*, and *ākhirah*, the beginning, this world, and the hereafter. *Āmīn. As-salāmu 'alaikum wa rahmatullāhi wa barakātuhu kulluhu.* May all the peace, the beneficence, and the blessings of God be upon you.

In the name of Allāh and the Rasūl ☺, I beg you to forgive me if anything I have said is wrong. Please forgive me if I have made any mistakes. I am only telling you what came to my *qalb*. I am only telling you what I understand in my *qalb*, my inner heart.

I humbly ask the great, the wise, and the *'ulamā'*, teachers, to do this. If there is any fault in what I have said, please forgive me for the sake of Allāh and the Rasūl ☺. *As-salāmu 'alaikum wa rahmatullāhi wa barakātuhu kulluhu.*

CHAPTER SEVEN

THE LAWS OF *JIHĀD*, *HOLY WAR*

Allāhu *Akbar*

God is most great

Do not kill someone, shouting, "Allāhu *akbar!* Allāhu *akbar!*" Instead, lead him to the good path, the straight path, and say, "Allāhu *akbar*, Allāh, You are the greatest."…He is the Almighty One who can create and destroy within the blinking of an eye. Allāh can do things before we even think of them. Life and death belong to Him, not to us.

THE LAWS OF *JIHĀD,* HOLY WAR

I seek refuge in Allāh from the accursed satan.
In the name of Allāh, the Most Compassionate, the Most Merciful.

My brothers and sisters in *Īmān*-Islam, let us speak some more on the meaning of *jihād,* holy war.

If we understand the Qur'ān properly, and if we understand the *hadīth,* the traditional stories of the Prophet 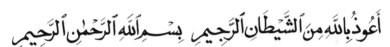, then Islām will be the water of *rahmah,* grace, for the entire world. It will cleanse everyone of their dirt and quench their thirst. It will make all *qalbs,* hearts, peaceful and be the very pulse of life, the heart-beat for all the children of Adam ﷺ, for all of creation.

A Hadīth Qudsī: A Direct Revelation to the Rasūlullāh ﷺ

The Exalted Prophet ﷺ, his companions, and his followers were attacked by those who did not accept Allāh or His Messenger. With forbearance and contentment, Muhammad ﷺ tolerated all the suffering that came to him. He conveyed to his followers the patience and the trust in Allāh that was given to him. However, eventually it became necessary to escape from this persecution, and he and his followers fled to Medina. Many of the people of Medina accepted the Rasūlullāh ☹, and there the Prophet ☹ and his followers found some peace. But a few hypocrites and troublemakers traveled between the two cities, spreading rumors, backbiting, and creating enmity. "The people of Mecca want to fight you," they told the Prophet ☹ and his followers. "They are destroying your homes and your property back there. They are killing your wives and children and injuring your brothers."

Upon hearing these stories, some of the companions complained to the Prophet ☹, pleading, "O Rasūl, they are causing us so much suffering! They have harmed our families, taken our possessions, destroyed our homes, and chased us from place to place. Now they are calling us cowards for running away. But we are courageous warriors, who must live with honor and dignity. We have accepted this disgrace long enough. Now we must fight.

"You are the Rasūl of Allāh. *Dunyā* and *ākhirah*, this world and the hereafter, are one to you, and Allāh is sufficient for you as your only wealth. So you are not concerned if people try to disgrace you, but in our state we cannot bear this. We need the means to live in this *dunyā* as well as in *ākhirah*. The Meccans have destroyed our houses, our property, and our relations. We must fight to regain our possessions; our hearts are hurt and we are suffering."

The companions of the Rasūl ☹ pleaded like this time after time, but the Rasūl ☹ did not grant them permission to fight. In his heart he was crying. The light in his eyes looked towards Allāh and his hands were outstretched asking for Allāh's *daulah*, the wealth of His divine knowledge and perfect faith. He spent every second in this state, asking Allāh to find ways to change the hearts of these people. The only sword in his hand was the sword of love, of *īmān* and unity, the sword of *sabūr*, inner patience, *shukūr*, contentment, *tawakkul*, trust in God, and *al-hamdu lillāh*, praise of God.

After a while, Hamzah ⓐ came with the same request, but the Rasūl ⓐ would not yield to him either. He would not tell his followers to begin *jihād*. Instead, he always answered, "You cannot do this without Allāh's permission, and Allāh has not granted it. Therefore, I cannot give you my permission, either. The true *jihād* of Islām is to wage war against our *nafs*, base desires, against all those aspects within ourselves which are the real enemies to our life in the *ākhirah*."

Still his companions pleaded, "We are warriors, and we have been disgraced. How can we live in this world with such dishonor?"

Then, while the Rasūl ⓐ was silent, Allāh's answer came. "O Muhammad, tell your *as-hāb* to begin the *jihād* in their hearts, to sacrifice the evils in their own *qalbs*. Your companions need to understand this."

So the Rasūl ⓐ conveyed this to his companions. "My brothers, Allāh has said that if you want to begin *jihād*, your first duty is to wage a holy war against the army of enemies that harm you from within. Each one of you must make your heart *halāl*, you must make your heart pure according to God's law, by performing the *qurbān* and sacrificing the evils which come to destroy it. You must perform the *qurbān* on all the things that veil your heart. You must make your *qalb* light. Nourish it with the food of Light which is the Treasure of Allāh, and avoid all that is opposite or *harām*, forbidden."

Allāh told the Rasūl ⓐ, "Only one who partakes of My food will have his hunger and his *nafs*, desires, appeased. The *halāl*, permissible, food for the *qalb* consists of My qualities, My actions, My *'ilm*, divine knowledge, My ninety-nine *wilāyats*, powers, My patience, My contentment, the surrender of *tawakkul*, and the praise of *al-hamdu lillāh*. Only such praise will end his hunger.

With My angels I will protect anyone who makes this intention the light within his heart, anyone who understands each of these qualities, anyone in whom the three thousand gracious qualities emerge.

"O Muhammad, I will reveal to you the angels that will come to protect you from the armies of Habīb ibn Mālik, sent by Abū Jahl. Each angel will have three thousand heads and six thousand hands, with the weapons appropriate to them. You will be able to see them all. Even if you are afraid, O Muhammad, go forward. You need not fear when you are in a state of *Īmān*-Islām. You have this *du'ā'*, the grace of My protection, the only true protection. I am the only One who can protect you in this way. Those who keep Me as their Protector will never be destroyed by anything in the world, but those who do not seek My help will be destroyed. As long as they have the *dunyā*, world, within them, they will be destroyed by that world. It is the *dunyā* which kills the *dunyā*. That is certain. Tell this to your followers.

"The *dunyā* does not belong to you, O Muhammad. You are here to realize Me. That is why I showed you My *wilāyats*, My actions, and that is why I created all My creations and their secrets. They are all examples I gave you so that you could understand Me. I am the only One who can perform these duties of creating, protecting, nourishing, giving food, and dispensing judgment. No one else can perform these *wilāyats*.

"O Muhammad, through Adam, through My creations, through the earth, the sky, the sun, the moon, the stars, fire, water, air, and the clouds, I have revealed My secrets. I sent you to teach your followers. Through you, I sent them so many words, so many actions, so many holy verses, and so much wisdom. I told you, 'Go even unto China to learn *'ilm*, divine knowledge, so that you would realize the value of *'ilm*. I gave the verses of the

Holy Qur'ān into your hands so that you could understand the connection between Myself and *insān,* and through this connection understand your earnings in this world and in the hereafter. The nature of your true wealth is explained in the Holy Qur'ān.

"Muhammad, you have revealed My word. If your followers want to learn the glory of the Qur'ān, if they want to understand its *daulah,* wealth, they must have the wisdom of *'ilm.* The Qur'ān is the *sirr,* secret, within the *sirr,* the *dhāt,* essence, within the *dhāt,* wisdom within wisdom, grace within grace, the *rūh,* soul, within the *rūh,* the *qalb,* innermost heart, within the *qalb,* the light within the light of the eye, the ear within the ear, the nose within the nose, the tongue within the tongue, and *'ilm* within *'ilm.* The Qur'ān is the *sūrah,* form, that exists within the *sūrah.* They must go within to know its real meaning.

"Tell your followers that anyone who is under My protection can never be destroyed, but anyone who leaves My protection and My help to wage *jihād* now, will destroy himself. Tell them that if one man seeks to kill or overcome another man, it is his own brothers that he will be destroying. They, in turn, will destroy him. Man has the choice of turning into a beast or becoming like his *Rabb,* his Lord. He has the potential to become *insān kāmil,* a true realized being. If he becomes Adam, then I will correct his faults and protect him, just as I protected Adam.

"Muhammad, tell this to your followers. They were all in darkness and torpor before they knew you. I made them come out of hiding and follow you, did I not? Earlier they were hidden in satan, but now they are your *as-hāb,* your companions. Now they are your warriors, but who were they before? What were their actions earlier compared to their actions now?

"With My words, you led them out of the darkness, and they began to follow you. They began to follow Me, their *Rabb,* their

Creator, did they not? Are they your enemies now? No, they have lost themselves and dedicated their lives to you and to Me. Earlier they were just like the people against whom they now want to wage war. They were just like these children of Adam. They were hidden in the same darkness, entangled in the same illusion, the same *nafs,* desires, and *siddhis,* elemental miracles. And they too were buried within satan. Therefore, would it be right to destroy others who are in that darkness now?

"Abū Bakr, 'Umar ibnul-Khattāb, 'Uthmān, and Hamzah[1] were all hidden in darkness. Look how they emerged. Tell your followers that rather than waging *jihād,* they should try to bring such people out of the darkness and make them understand Allāh. Instead of fighting against them, they should help them accept the truth, strengthen their *īmān,* and try to change them.

"To convert without force is the way of Islām. To destroy and kill and slaughter people is not Islām. Therefore, tell your followers to wage *jihād* by lifting up those who have fallen into the state of *kufr,* disbelief. That is Islām. Tell them to use My actions, My words, and My behavior in order to release those who are hidden in satan and buried in illusion. That is the true *jihād.* Reveal this to your followers." This is what Allāh told the Rasūl ⊕.

Allāh could have destroyed all the unbelievers, but instead He brought them forth from the darkness. This is the true *jihād:* to convert without force. In this way, Allāh's commandments came to show justice. This is Islām.

---

1. Abū Bakr as-Siddīq ⊕: The first caliph and a father-in-law to the Prophet ⊕.
   'Umar ibnul-Khattāb ⊕: The second caliph and a father-in-law to the Prophet ⊕. At first he was violently opposed to Muhammad ⊕, but later heard his sister reciting part of the Qur'ān and was overcome. Going directly to Muhammad ⊕, he professed his belief in Allāh and His Prophet ⊕.
   'Uthmān ⊕: The third caliph; compiled the verses of the Qur'ān and produced the authorized version which is still in existence.
   Hamzah ⊕: Paternal uncle and foster brother of the Prophet ⊕.

But not all of the followers of Muhammad ☻ were able to attain this state. Some did not have the inner strength of *sabūr*, *shukūr*, and *tawakkulun ʿalAllāh*. They were not able to say, "*In shā'Allāh.* If God wills," and "*Mā shā'Allāh.* Whatever God wills." And they continued to plead, "Let us ruin those who try to ruin us. O Rasūl, we are not like you, we are ordinary people just like they are. We need to fight force with force." The Rasūl ☻ tried to teach them patience, but they had this need in their hearts.

Finally Allāh said, "All right, tell them to begin their *jihād.*" As they were preparing for battle, certain restrictions were placed upon them. They were told, "Do not fight this war for the sake of your pride, to show that you are a warrior or that you are strong. Fight only against those who come to fight with you. You may engage in combat only with someone who has taken your possessions. You must not usurp the possessions of another. You must not touch their women or harm their children. You must not destroy their houses or their farms and crops or kill their livestock. You must not cut down their trees, destroy the countryside, or ruin their wells. You must not kill those who run away in fear, and you must not strike someone who falls down in battle. Only if someone comes at you with a sword in his hand may you defend yourself."

The Rasūl ☻ conveyed the rules to ʿAlī [2] and to Abū Bakr as-Siddīq, may Allāh be pleased with them. "Go and fight," the Rasūl ☻ said, "but do not go beyond these limits. If you fail to obey these rules, you will be great sinners. If you wage war for the sake of land, houses, possessions, or happiness, forgetting the rules that I have given, then you will be blamed and you will be

---

2. ʿAlī ☻: The fourth caliph, son-in-law of the Prophet Muhammad ☻, husband of Fātimah ☻ and father of Hasan ☻ and Husain ☻. The second convert to Islām, following Khadījah ☻, the first wife of the Prophet ☻.

questioned on the Day of *Qiyāmah*. Allāh established all these restrictions and then told Muhammad ☺, "Tell them to go in this
state and regain what is rightfully theirs."

This was the state in which *jihād* was waged during the time
of the Prophet ☺. Even so, the Rasūlullāh ☺ did not take part
in these battles. He instead spent the entire time praying for the
fighting to stop. He remained alone, hands outstretched, praying
to Allāh. Every second his heart was crying, and the light in his
eyes was directed towards Allāh.

"Change their hearts," he prayed. "Fill them with Your love
and grace. Give them unity. Let them drop the swords from their
hands and raise the sword of *īmān*. O Allāh, make them accept
You, make them praise You and pray to You. Give them that certitude and love."

The only sword that ever touched the Rasūl's ☺ hands was the
sword of *īmān*, of *sabur, shukūr, tawakkul, al-hamdu lillāh,* the
sword of love and of the unity of brotherhood. We must think
about this.

A Story of 'Alī ☺

One day when 'Alī ☺ was in battle, his opponent's sword
broke and the man fell. 'Alī ☺ stood above him, holding his sword
to the man's chest, and said, "If you had a sword in your hand, I
would continue this fight. But since your sword is broken, I cannot strike you."

The man replied, "If I had a sword at this moment, I would
cut off your arms and legs."

"All right," 'Alī ☺ replied, and handed the man his sword.

"What are you doing?" the man asked. "I am your enemy, am
I not?"

'Alī ☺ looked him in the eye and said, "You swore that if you had a sword in your hand you would kill me. Now you have my sword, so go ahead and strike me." The man could not. "That was your ignorance and arrogance speaking," 'Alī ⊕ explained. "In the realm of Allāh, there is no fight or enmity between you and me. We are brethren. The real war is between the truth and your lack of wisdom; it is between truth and falsehood. You and I are just watching that battle. You are my brother. If I were to harm you at this point, I would have to answer for it on the Day of *Qiyāmah*. Allāh would question me about it."

"Is this the way of Islam?" the man asked.

"Yes," 'Alī ⊕ replied. "These are the words of Allāh, the All-Powerful, Unique One."

Immediately the man bowed down at 'Alī's ⊕ feet and begged, "Teach me the *kalimah*," and 'Alī ⊕ taught him. "*Lā ilāha illAllāhu.* "There is no God but Allāh."

The same thing happened during a later battle. 'Alī ⊕ felled his opponent, placed his foot on the man's chest, and held a sword to his neck. Again he could not kill the man.

"Why don't you kill me?" the man shouted angrily. "I am your enemy. Why are you just standing there?" and he spit in 'Alī's ⊕ face.

At first 'Alī ⊕ became angry. Then he removed his foot from the man's chest and put aside his sword. "I am not your enemy," 'Alī ⊕ replied. "The real enemies are the evil qualities within us. You are my brother, yet you spit in my face. When you spat on me, I became angry. The arrogance of the "I" came to me. If I had killed you when I was in that state, then I would be a sinner, a murderer. I would have become the very thing I was fighting against. That crime would be recorded against my name, and I would have to answer for it later, when Allāh questions me. That is why I cannot slay you."

"Then there is no fight between you and me?" the man asked.

"No. The battle is between wisdom and ignorance, between truth and falsehood," 'Alī ☺ told him. "Even though you spat on me and taunted me to kill you, I cannot."

"Where did such a rule come from?"

"These are the rules of Allāh. This is Islām."

Immediately, the man fell before 'Alī's ☺ feet, and he too was taught the *kalimah.*

This is the difference between the ways of Allāh and the ways of the world. There are two kinds of *jihād.* The real battle is within, but even in an outer war, there are rules. Those who fight the inner war follow Allāh's rules, but those who fight for the sake of wife, children, or house follow other rules. If even an atom's worth of such thoughts are present, it is not true *jihād,* but rather, a political war. It is fought for the sake of land and country, not for the sake of Allāh. With wisdom, we must understand what the true *jihād* is, and we must think about the answers we will have to give on the Day of Questioning.

The Rasūl ☺ and his followers had certitude, unity, justice, and conscience. It was in this state that their *jihād* was waged and the battles of Badr and Uhud were fought. Some people were killed, but after these battles peace reigned in Islām. The *salām,* the greeting of peace, and the *salawāt,* the glorification of Allāh and the Rasūl ☺, and the words Allāhu *akbar,* God is most great, resonated throughout the land. Finally, it was in this state that Mecca was captured. The Rasūl ☺ returned to Mecca, not with the sword, but with Allāh's praise.

We must understand this. Mecca was not conquered with the

sword but with *Īmān*-Islām, with love, compassion, unity, and faith, with *sabūr*, patience, *shukūr*, contentment, *tawakkul*, trust in God, and *al-hamdu lillāh*, praise of God. It was through Allāh's qualities that Islām grew. It was these qualities that conquered the people.

Whatever is conquered by the sword does not last. The one who picks up the sword will one day die by that same sword. The one who picks up a gun will die by the gun. Whatever one raises in enmity, that very same weapon will cause his destruction. Whatever trick a man learns will one day bring about his destruction.

However, the one who receives the complete wealth of Allāh's love, compassion, and *īmān* will have *hayāh*, eternal life. That beauty of Islām and that resplendence will not die in *dunyā* or in *ākhirah*. The body of such a one will be different and he will be different. The body will belong to the world, but the qualities within him will belong to *ākhirah*, Allāh's kingdom. Even though he lives in this world, he will be like the lotus flower which grows in water yet does not keep the water within itself. He will live in this world, but the world will not be within him. Only Allāh's qualities and His beauty will exist there.

Reflect upon this. There is nothing that the All-Powerful One cannot do. Shedding blood is not the way. Instead, we must cut away our arrogance, karma, and illusion. We must cut away this darkness of ignorance and establish light. This is true *jihād*. This is the only way to spread wisdom and *'ilm*, divine knowledge.

Do not kill someone, shouting, "Allāhu *akbar!* Allāhu *akbar!*" Instead, lead him to the good path, the straight path, and say, "Allāhu *akbar.* Allāh, You are the greatest." That is *Īmān*-Islām. That is true *jihād*. To kill the inner enemy of truth is *Īmān*-Islām, but to kill an external enemy and say, "Allāhu *akbar*" is not Islām.

We have to think about this.

People shout, *"Jihād! Jihād!"* without any understanding, but that is not holy war. We should not spread Islām through the sword; we must spread it through the *kalimah,* through truth, *īmān,* and love.

If you believe in Allāh, the Unique, All-Pervasive Power, then His *salāms,* greetings of peace, His *salawāt,* blessings, His love, His compassion, His wisdom, His equality, His comfort, and His qualities will be your weapons of war. This is what was explained to the companions of the Rasūl ☺. It is with these weapons alone that we should make our *jihād.* These are the weapons of *tauhīd,* the state of oneness with God. These are the weapons of the All-Powerful, Unique One.

Do we really need to wage war against others for His sake? Do we really need to destroy others with swords? No, it is not necessary for us to destroy in this way. How can we accept the *kalimah* of the All-Powerful, Unique One if we do that? Instead, we need to discard what He has discarded. He is the Almighty One who can create and destroy within the blinking of an eye. Allāh can do things before we even think of them. Life and death belong to Him, not to us.

If we think about it, we will see that there are many explanations in the words of Allāh and the words of the Prophet ☺. We must understand the *'ilm* within the *'ilm* that exists in the *hadīth* and the Qur'ān. We cannot study only the surface meanings; we must dig deep to see what is within. For every issue, we must think, "What did the Exalted Prophet ☺ say about this? What revelations have been given about this? What has been said to the people of *'ilm* about this? What has been said to the *as-hāb,* the companions of the Prophet ☺, the ones with the clarity of wisdom? What has been said to the ones without wisdom?"

For each question there are many explanations that have been given. For each person's level of wisdom, an appropriate reply has been given. We need to understand the words of Allāh that were sent to us. That is *tauhīd*. If we understand the inner meaning of the words of Allāh, it will be good. There are so many enemies; there is this *jihād* within and there is the outer *jihād*. You need to think about this. My love you, my children.

Allāh's *jihād* is a good thing. We must raise His weapons of love, compassion, mercy, comfort, *sabūr,* and *shukūr.* Then we will have victory over everything. The other weapons are implements of destruction. Knives and swords will never bring victory; they can only destroy. Allāh's weapons never destroy.

My love you. *Āmīn.*

CHAPTER EIGHT

THE SPREAD
OF ISLĀM

Al-Īmān

Absolute faith, certitude, and determination

Īmān alone can capture another heart. *Īmān* alone can rule the world. The qualities of Allāh that exist within the *qalb,* inner heart, of one with *īmān* must reach out, enter the *qalb* of another, and give him comfort and peace. It is Allāh's compassion, His equality, tranquility, and peacefulness, His integrity, His honesty, and the manner in which He embraces and protects all lives with equal justice which can bring another being to the state of harmony and compel him to bow in unity. It is these qualities that can conquer people and countries.

CHAPTER EIGHT

THE SPREAD OF ISLĀM

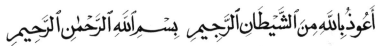

I seek refuge in Allāh from the accursed satan.
In the name of Allāh, the Most Compassionate, the Most Merciful.

*A*s-salāmu 'alaikum wa rahmatullāhi wa barakātuhu kulluhu. May all the peace, the beneficence, and blessings of God be upon you.

My brothers and sisters in Islām who are *mu'mins*, true believers, I give you my *salāms*, greetings. *As-salāmu 'alaikum*. May the peace of Allāh be upon you.

It has been 1,405 years since the congregation called Islām emerged from among the children of Adam ☺. Allāh, *subhānahu wa ta'ālā*, perfected this state called Islām with the coming of the Final Prophet, the Chosen Messenger, Muhammad Mustāfār-Rasūl, the Chosen Messenger ☺. Through the Angel Gabriel ☺, Allāh sent the Holy Qur'ān, the *Tiru Marai*, as revelations to His Prophet ☺. In turn, the Rasūl ☺ explained the five and six principles of Islām to the *qutbs*, the great holy men of divine wisdom; the *auliyā'*, the friends of God; the *malā'ikah*, the archangels; the *ambiyā'*, prophets; and to all mankind.

But Islām is not just 1,405 years old. Islām is truth. It is Allāh's radiant Light, His qualities and actions, His attributes, *wilāyats*, and His compassion. Islām is perfect purity. Allāh placed this purity within man when He created Adam ⊕. Islām, therefore, existed even before the creation of man. It existed in *arwāh*, the world of the pure souls. This has been revealed in the *hadīth*, the traditional stories of Islām.

Truth is one and Islām is one. It shows no differences between religions and sects, races and tribes, or between black and white or red and yellow; between people from China and people from Africa, America, Europe, Australia, Asia, Russia, or any country in the world. It does not show differences between those in the realm of *awwal,* the time of creation, and those in *ākhirah,* the hereafter. The word Islām has only one meaning: the unity and peacefulness of Truth. That Truth is Allāh. His three thousand gracious qualities and attributes, His unity, tranquility, and virtuous conduct, His equality, and His compassion—these are what comprise Islām. To conduct ourselves in the right manner, to know what is *halāl,* permissible, and to act accordingly, to know what is *harām,* forbidden, and to avoid it—this is what is called *īmān,* absolute faith, certitude, and determination.

Allāh rules all the universes through this *īmān,* and through this truth, this peacefulness, and these virtuous qualities and conduct. They are His *daulah,* wealth. And it is to attain this state that we recite the *ash-shahādah kalimah,* "*Ash-hadu al-lā ilāha il-lAllāhu wahdahu lā sharīka lah; wa ash-hadu anna Muhammadan 'abduhu wa rasūluh.* "There is no God but Allāh." He is One without a partner; and I witness that Muhammad is His slave and His Messenger." He is the One to whom we pray. He is the Truth which we must accept in *dunyā* and *ākhirah.*

My brothers who are *mu'mins,* true believers, we must realize this. Islām must realize this. There should be no divisions among those who, with *īmān*, have accepted the truth of Allāh and affirmed the *kalimah*. All those who worship Him and pray to Him should be in unity in prayer. All must unite as one in all states: in sorrow and in joy, in *maut*, death, and in *hayāh*, life, and in all three realms of *awwal*, *dunyā*, and *ākhirah*, the beginning, this world, and the hereafter. To be in Islām means to be united as one congregation even in *ākhirah*, seeing Him face to face, worshipping Him, and giving Him *salāms*. Here and in the hereafter, we must embrace all those who have *īmān*, all those who accept Allāh in their *qalbs*. We must pray to Allāh with this unity, peacefulness, and truth. We must give *salāms*, greetings of peace, to each brother. Standing face to face, our eyes looking directly into our brother's eyes, our hands clasping his hands, and our hearts embracing his heart with love, we must say, "*As-salāmu 'alaikum.* May the peace of God be upon you." This is the unity and beauty of Islām, the beauty that the Rasūl ☻ brought to the people.

Wherever we go, our *qalbs*, inner hearts, must be in that state. Our prayers must be one-pointed, directed towards the same place, towards Allāh, the One who is Truth. If every one of us can reflect on this, if we can recite the *salawāt*, praising Allāh and the Rasūl ☻, look each other in the eye, give *salāms*, and embrace each other, if every one of us can achieve that oneness of the *qalb* with all lives, then we will be *mu'mins*, true believers.

As brothers in Islām, as *mu'mins*, we must open our *qalbs* and look within. Without jealousy, envy, deceit, or trickery, without divisiveness or discrimination, we must turn our hearts to the straight path and perform *tasbīh*, glorifying Allāh. Accepting the truth and abiding by it, we must establish that truth, in the right manner, with love, forbearance, and equality. This is the state of *Īmān*-Islām, which the Rasūl ☻ brought 1,405 years ago. This is what is spoken of in the Qur'ān.

My brothers, before the time of the Rasūl ☺, there were many, many divisions and sects among the people of Mecca. They worshipped 360 different idols, which they housed in the Ka'bah. They performed mantras and magics, *siddhis* and miracles. Even though so many prophets had come: Adam, Noah, Abraham, Ishmael, Moses, and many others, peace be upon them all, Mecca was still a place of idol worship.

Before the time of the Rasūl ☺, it was possible to refer to those who had no *īmān* as *kāfirs*, unbelievers. That was the word that the world used. All the people who lived in Mecca and Medina were *kāfirs*, before the Prophet ☺ came and taught them the *ash-shahādah kalimah*. But did Islām reject the people of Mecca and Medina? No. It was not the purpose of the Rasūl ☺ to divide or create enmity. Islām tells us not to discard the *kāfirs*, but to transform them. Once they acquire *īmān*, once they have faith and their *qalbs* are filled with light, once they perform their prayers to Allāh alone, they too will be in Islām.

All those in Islām must reflect on this today. If we consider the way in which the Prophet ☺ transformed the people of Mecca and Medina, can we not follow that same process now, in the rest of the world? Islām is compassion, tolerance, forbearance, and the gracious qualities of Allāh. It does not create barriers or divide people; it shows them the way and invites them into itself. That was the way of the Rasūl ☺ and the earlier prophets.

Just as the Prophet ☺ transformed the *kāfirs*, those who reject faith in Allāh, into Islām through his love and his gracious qualities, each one of you must first turn those disbelieving qualities within yourself into good qualities. You must develop *sabūr*, inner patience, *shukūr*, contentment, *tawakkul*, trust in Allāh, and *al-hamdu lillāh*, praise of Allāh. Only then can you truly be a follower of Islām.

It is these good qualities and good thoughts that can attract and capture the heart of another. It is this love that can open and reveal a person's innermost heart to himself. Once that *qalb* is opened, *īmān* and faith can bring him to a state of steadfastness. That person is then ready to go in search of the Truth, and when he finds the Truth, he finds Allāh who is that Truth. Once he finds the justice and the peacefulness of Allāh, he too will be able to dispense justice and peacefulness throughout the world. In this state, he will recite *tasbīh* to Allāh, glorifying the Protector, the Rahmān, the Most Compassionate. Such a man will embrace and comfort others with his life, his *qalb,* and his body. This is how the heart, the world, and Allāh's kingdom of justice can be ruled by the qualities which emerge from the *qalb* of one who has *īmān.*

You should not call anyone an unbeliever. When your love goes out and embraces the hearts of others, when truth enters their hearts and *īmān* conquers them, at that moment, at the very instant that faith appears in their *qalbs,* they are in Islam, are they not? They have turned around and hoisted the flag of Islam, have they not? They have accepted Allāh as the Truth. Those whom you called unbelievers have changed. Now they worship Allāh. This is how the *rahmah* called *īmān* reaches out, overcomes, and conquers them. With good qualities, peacefulness, and patience, it comforts others and brings peace to their *qalbs.*

Īmān alone can capture another heart. *Īmān* alone can rule the world. The qualities of Allāh that exist within the *qalb,* inner heart, of one with *īmān* must reach out, enter the *qalb* of another, and give him comfort and peace. It is Allāh's compassion, His equality, tranquility, and peacefulness, His integrity, His honesty, and the manner in which He embraces and protects all lives with equal justice which can bring another being to the state of harmony and compel him to bow in unity. It is these qualities that can conquer people and countries. First they capture the hearts of a few, then they reach out to all those in the village, then the city, and eventually these qualities reach out to the entire population of the country. Through Allāh, *īmān* conquers *awwal, dunyā, ākhirah,* the beginning, this world, the hereafter, and all of everything. This is the proof that Allāh alone rules His kingdom, and this is how true Islām spreads. There should be no wars to conquer other lands. The war is within oneself, fighting one's own qualities. If we can complete this war, then our *īmān* can conquer other hearts and other countries. It is only Allāh's qualities, His virtuous conduct and behavior that can rule *dunyā* and *ākhirah.* We must perfect these qualities within ourselves.

To be in Islām is to act according to the good qualities of virtue, modesty, compassion, peacefulness, forbearance, Allāh's three thousand gracious attributes, His unity, His tranquility, and His equality. Islām embraces all equally in both joy and sorrow. If one is hungry, all are hungry. If one is sad, all are sad. If one is happy, all are happy.

Joining together and talking about these things is not the true voice of Islām. Islām is not idle talk. We must bring these words into our hearts. To give voice to Islām is to realize this state and make it steadfast within us, and then to act accordingly. To praise Allāh saying, "*Al-hamdu lillāh.* All praise is to You," to recite the *salawāt* in praise of His prophets, and to greet those of *īmān* with, "*As-salāmu 'alaikum.* May the peace of God be upon you"—that is the true voice of Islām. To come together to offer *tasbīh,* glorifying Allāh alone, is Islām.

We who are in *Īmān*-Islām, we who are *mu'mins,* our entire generation must reflect upon this. We must understand the words of Allāh, the words of the Rasūl ☻, and the treasure of grace buried within the Qur'ān. We must embrace that treasure to our *qalb* before we can explain it to the *qalbs* of others and bring them to accept it. The Qur'ān is the treasury, the wealth of Islām, from which everything comes.

We must always show *sabūr*, inner patience, *shukūr*, contentment, *tawakkul*, trust in God, and we must praise God, saying, "*Al-hamdu lillāh*." Whatever suffering we face, we must have *sabūr*. If we undergo even greater suffering, we must have *shukūr*. If we undergo still greater difficulty, we must surrender, saying, "*Tawakkalnā 'alAllāh*, we surrender and give all responsibility to God." And when our suffering extends yet further, beyond our endurance, we can do nothing but praise Him, saying, "*Al-hamdu lillāh*." This is Islām—to praise Allāh for whatever happens.

In this state of *Īmān*-Islām, if we have a quarrel with somebody in the *waqt* of 'asr, the afternoon prayer, we must make peace, embrace each other, and give *salāms* by the *waqt* of *maghrib*, the early evening prayer. Any evil influences created in one *waqt* must be thrown away by the next time of prayer. This is the state of Islām as lived by *mu'mins*.

For the faults we committed before the present *waqt*, we must ask God for forgiveness and strive for repentance, *taubah*. For what is happening now, during this *waqt*, during this very breath, we must proclaim *tasbīh* to Him, glorifying His name. And for the next breath, for the next *waqt* which is to come, we must surrender, saying, "*Tawakkalnā 'alAllāh*. Whether or not we are alive in the next moment is Allāh's will. May His will be fulfilled." If we have this faith with perfect certitude, if we have this intention with every breath, if we can acquire His qualities and His actions, then that is Islām.

To worry about what has happened before or what is to come later is not Islām. If one constantly worries about what has gone by, his *qalb* will be filled with grief and darkness. Grief and darkness are not Islām. Envy, jealousy, and treachery are not Islām. For what has gone by, all we can do is ask forgiveness and strive for repentance, *taubah,* and then complete whatever needs to be done in this present *waqt.* This is the correct state of Islām, the state that an *insān* who is a *mu'min* must attain.

If our *qalbs* attain this state of clarity, we will never see any differences anywhere. We will never show any discrimination anywhere. Allāh does not see any differences. Truth has no differences, and the prayer that accepts Allāh as the only One who is worthy of worship shows no divisions. There is no discrimination among the gracious attributes of Allāh. There is no discrimination in His equality and His peacefulness. And once His qualities develop in us, we too will not see any differences.

Islām brings that compassion, that equality, and that peacefulness to every heart and demonstrates that unity to every *qalb.* May we reflect on this. If each one of us can establish this state, if each of us can exhibit and prove this within our own *qalbs,* we will be *mu'mins,* true believers. To be in Islām we must bring these qualities into action within us. This is the command of Allāh, shown to us by every prophet He sent, from Adam ☻ to the Rasūl ☻.

May we who have the *īmān* of *mu'mins* think deeply about this. May every *qalb* reflect on this. The kings who are *mu'mins,* the elders who are *mu'mins,* those with the *daulah,* wealth of Allāh, who are *mu'mins,* the rulers, the learned ones, and the *'ulamā',* teachers, who are *mu'mins*—everyone must reflect on this. There is a difference between the poor and the rich in this world; even though we may be poor here, we can earn the *daulah* of Allāh in *ākhirah,* the hereafter. The wealth of this world will be left behind, but the wealth in *ākhirah* will remain with us forever.

Those who acquire the wealth which consists of His qualities, His actions, and the *'ilm*, divine knowledge, of His *rahmah*, grace; those who have learned that *'ilm* and have put it into practice; those who have made their *qalbs* the repository of this wealth of Allāh's grace—they are the ones who can truly be called the wealthy ones in *ākhirah*.

May this *rahmah*, this beneficence which Allāh has given, fill the *qalbs* of everyone around us. May their hearts be filled with the wealth of Allāh's grace in all three realms of *awwal, dunyā,* and *ākhirah*, the time of creation, this world, and the hereafter. May they be filled with the wealth of *gnānam*, grace-awakened wisdom; the wealth of prayer and worship, *'ibādah;* and the wealth of justice. May we make our *qalbs* the repository of Allāh's *daulah* and share it with the *qalbs* of our brothers. May we strive hard to help them fill their *qalbs* with this *daulah* of *'ilm* and *īmān*, so that they will be the wealthy ones in *ākhirah*. May all attain that peace within their *qalbs*. May we make every effort to do this. In our prayer, in our congregations, in the mosques, in our jobs, in our worldly life, in death and in life, in joy and in sorrow—may we strive for only this wealth, this unity, this *rahmah*, grace.

My very precious brothers who have opened out the umbrella of grace called Islām, unfurled the flag of *īmān*, and walked on the good path—with awareness in our *qalbs*, let us establish this state of unity called Islām and lead our lives in that unity. *Āmīn*.

Certain words may have been repeated here, but they contain several meanings which must be said over and over and over again until they are understood. They have been repeated so that we will gain more and more understanding each time we read them. Therefore, please forgive this repetition. Please forgive us in the name of Allāh and the Rasūl ⊕. These are the words that came to our heart. Please do not reject them.

If there is any fault, please forgive me in the name of Allāh and the Rasūl ☺. I give my *salāms,* greetings of peace, to all of you.

As-salāmu ʿalaikum wa rahmatullāhi wa barakātuhu kulluhu. May all the peace, the beneficence, and the blessings of God be upon you. *Āmīn.*

May Allāh guide us on the path of equality and peacefulness. May He strengthen our *īmān,* take us on the straight path, and accept us. *Āmīn.*

PART THREE

UNITY

UNITY
The Secret of Creation

Al-Ittihād

Unity

We must make all people one with us. The Rasūl ﷺ explained this to us, but some of us who came to the world forgot what Allāh said. We must learn to wash away our separations and become one again. That is true Islām.

UNITY
The Secret of Creation

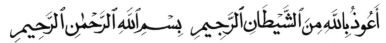

I seek refuge in Allāh from the accursed satan.
In the name of Allāh, the Most Compassionate, the Most Merciful.

To Allāh alone belongs the responsibility for the beginning and the end of all things. Only He knows the secrets of all the creations of the eighteen thousand universes. May we praise only Him. *Āmīn.*

In this world, Allāh created so many different kinds of beautiful and valuable things. But there would have been no creation at all if the five elements had not come together in unity. Earth, fire, water, air, and ether are enemies to one another, but God joined them together through the *ash-shahādah kalimah.*[1] He made them one through *Nūr Muhammad,* saying, "*Yā* Muhammad, without you I would not have created anything. I have created everything through you."

Everything created out of the joining of these five energies is *haif,*[2] harmful. It contains some imperfection or some weakness

---

1. The Second *Kalimah,* the affirmation of faith. See Appendix.
2. *haif* (A) Wrong, injustice, harm, damage, prejudice.

that can cause harm. Everything other than Allāhu taʿālā, the All-Knowing and Almighty God, is imperfect and will change. If we consider all that can be destroyed and all that cannot, we will see that Allāhu taʿālā Nāyan is the only One who is eternal, the only One who lives forever.

Before the five elements recited the *ash-shahādah kalimah* and joined together, each one proclaimed with great pride, "I! I! There is no one greater than I! I can do anything I want." Water said, "I can do anything I want." Air said, "I can do anything I want." Earth, fire, and ether also said, "I can do anything I want." To break their pride, to destroy their arrogance, and to bring them together, God showed them their weaknesses.

To earth He said, "Do not think that you are great. Good and evil and all that is filthy and discarded exist within you. And everyone steps on you."

"I am indeed *haif,*" the earth had to admit.

"Recite the *kalimah* in the name of the Light of *Nūr Muhammad,*" God commanded. And earth recited the *kalimah.*

Then God told water, "You wash away dirt from others, but then you keep it all within yourself, and the millions of worms and insects and germs that grow within you make you smell terrible. Furthermore, you have no shape of your own; you are trapped by what surrounds you. Only when there is an opening can you flow out and escape. O water, how can you say that you are great when you can be pushed about by winds and blocked by earth from going wherever you want?"

"I am *haif,*" admitted water.

"Recite the *kalimah* in the name of the Light of *Nūr Muhammad,*" God commanded. And water recited the *kalimah.*

Then God told fire, "You think you can do whatever you want, but air can blow you out and water can drown you. That should put an end to your arrogance. There is only One who is without *haif*, without injustice. That One is Allāh, the eternal One who has no beginning or end."

And fire also had to admit, "I am *haif*."

"Recite the *kalimah* in the name of the Light of *Nūr Muhammad*," commanded God. And fire recited the *kalimah*.

Next God told air, "You look at everyone's face, but no one looks at your face. You think you are great, but there are tall mountain ranges that can block you. And when houses, trees, or mountains stand in your way, what can you do? Nothing."

"I am *haif*," admitted air.

"Then recite the *kalimah* and know that there is someone greater than you. That One is Allāh." And air recited the *kalimah*.

Then God told ether, "You are maya, you are illusion. You are nothing but glitters. One storm pushes you this way, the next pushes you that way. As soon as daylight comes your glitters disappear and the beauty of your own light fades. You are powerless in the daylight."

"I am *haif*," admitted ether.

"Recite the *kalimah*," God commanded. And ether recited the *kalimah*.

So when the five affirmed their faith, *īmān*, in *Nūr Muhammad* and said the *kalimah* in the name of the Light of *Nūr Muhammad*, they became one, and Islām came into being. Only when they recited the *kalimah* did they join together in unity; that unity within all creation is Islām.

After joining the five elements, God created Adam ☺ and all that exists. Everything was created in unity. Adam ☺ and Eve ☺ had twenty-one sets of twins, but instead of living together in unity, they separated from each other and scattered throughout the land. They began to form separate languages by imitating the voices of birds, animals, and other sounds in their different environments. As centuries passed, mankind developed more and more differences and forgot the meaning of Islām.

Islām came as unity, for the beginning and for the end. It came through the Rasūl ☻, through *Nūr Muhammad,* through *Ahmad,* through the Muhammad ☻ of the nine meanings.[3] When Allāh said, "*Yā* Muhammad, without you I would not have created anything, then or now," He was speaking about that Light of Muhammad ☻ which has existed as Islām since the time of *arwāh,* the world of the souls, and which will exist forever. He was not referring to something that came with the Prophet Muhammad ☻ 1,407 years ago. If Islām only began on that date, then what happened to all the prophets and all the people who came before that?

In any time, all those who attain the clarity of Islām reach heaven. In the time of Adam ☻, people worshipped like Hindus. Were they sent to hell? Did God send Adam ☻ to hell? So many yugas and eons have passed since then, so many people have come and gone. Did they all go to hell? No, those who understood and attained clarity in the past were certainly within Islām and were *mu'mins,* true believers. They reached *firdaus,* the eighth heaven. The Light of Muhammad ☻ existed as Islām in the beginning as it will in the end. God has been teaching the people step by step,

---

3. The nine meanings refer to nine names of Muhammad ☻: *Anāthi Muhammad* (the unmanifested); *Āthi Muhammad* (the manifested); *Awwal Muhammad* (the beginning, the emergence of creation); *Hayāt Muhammad* (the *rūh,* the emergence of the soul); *An'am Muhammad* (the *rizq,* the food or nourishment, for all creations); *Ahmad* (the *qalb,* the innermost heart); *Muhammad* (the beauty in the face, a reflection of the beauty of the heart); *Nūr Muhammad* (the plenitude, the Light which became completeness within Allāh and emerged); *Allāh Muhammad* (The Light of Allāh within *Muhammad,* and the Light of *Muhammad* within Allāh).

sending the prophets one after another, each with a message, each with revelations for a particular time.

God has said that man is the most exalted among His creation, because he has *pahut arivu,* divine analytic wisdom. If he becomes a *mu'min,* a true believer, he can know and see things that the heavenly beings cannot. God gave the jinns and fairies only thirty-six powers, but to man He has given ninety-six. Beyond these powers are *insān,* Muhammad ☮, *Nūr,* and Allāh. First: when wisdom resplends, that is *insān,* the human being, *sūratul-*Adam ☮, the form of Adam ☮. Second: when the heart, *aham,* becomes radiant and shines in the face, *muham,* as the beauty of that face, that is Muhammad ☮. Third: when the light of wisdom becomes complete and ever present, that is the beauty of the *Nūr,* the effulgence of Muhammad ☮. And fourth: when we block off everything else and stand in silence as the *alif,*[4] with our hands folded in *takbīr,*[5] that is Allāh, resplending as Wisdom, the One who makes silent things speak and makes them visible within.

Insān, Muhammad ☮, *Nūr,* and Allāh: these four, with the ninety-six powers, represent the one hundred names. God gave all but one of these names to man so that he could bring them into action. That one name, Allāh, He kept for Himself. He is the One who never diminishes, the One who cannot be compared to anything. Allāh is not like anything else. We can cut a rough stone, wash it, facet it, and compare its value with that of other stones, but Allāh cannot be compared with any of His creations. He is without price, without comparison. He is the most valuable Treasure of all. That Treasure is concealed within man. A man could not even move if Allāh were not within him. A true man is

---

4. *alif* (A) The first letter of the Arabic alphabet which to the transformed man represents Allāh.

5. *takbīr* (A) To say, "Allāhu *akbar,* God is great," in prayer.

within Allāh, hidden within Him, surrendered to Him. The true man keeps Allāh within himself and Allāh keeps that man within Him.

Allāh created truth and the light of truth. He also created flower gardens with different kinds of flowers and so many precious gems with different kinds of light. He created Adam ☉, without whom no human beings would exist, for man came from Adam ☉. Some of Allāh's creations who came in the form of men behave like animals, while some who came in the form of animals behave like men. An animal or even a satan can be like a man, and a man can be like an animal or a satan. There are such things as evil beings.

Allāh made all of His creations as one, but some of them have separated and become soiled. That does not mean we should discard them, saying, "They do this, they do that. They are not like us. They must be kept separate." Instead we must wash away the dirt and become one. If a man's shirt gets splashed with mud by a car, does that make it a different shirt? We cannot say that. It is the same shirt that he bought, and if he washes it, it will return to its original state. He does not throw it out and say, "This has changed. This is something else. This is different."

Similarly, you do not discard someone because he falls and smells bad. You should wash him with the *ash-shahādah kalimah,* with wisdom and with *īmān,* with unity and with good qualities. When the time comes, he will wash himself and become clean. What can we show him in the meantime? Love. Our love must be like soap. If we show the qualities of compassion, love, charity, generosity, justice, and peace, that will bring him along.

We are not Muslims if we discard someone saying, "He holds another belief. He belongs to a different religion. His color is not like ours." Color does not matter; what we need is to be one.

The only real difference between men lies in their conduct and actions, their qualities, and their *īmān*. When these are correct, then men are one, with no differences. We must keep the good things and wash away the dirt. We must wash our *qalbs* until they become light. We must make all people one with us. The Rasūl ☺ explained this to us, but some of us who came to the world forgot what Allāh said. We must learn to wash away our separations and become one again. That is true Islām. True Islām has never discarded anyone. Once we entrust the *kalimah* to Allāh, we will never again perceive anyone as different from us. We will begin to love our neighbors as ourselves.

We must stop looking at the outside. We must stop looking at things like colors. If you peel off the skin of a dog, its flesh will look the same as that of a deer. If you peel off the skin of a pig, its flesh might look like that of a goat. You may not even be able to tell the difference between the flesh of a goat and the flesh of a child. All flesh is the same color, only the skin looks different. No matter what color a lampshade is there will still be light. Light is always light. Truth and good qualities are the light in our hearts, and that light must shine within.

We have to look beyond what we see on the outside. A person may have strayed from the path or may follow some other religion, but he is still our neighbor. We have to understand that people worship in many ways. Hindus may call themselves *saivam*, which means purity. There are many different names for purity. Buddhists acknowledge purity, yet they say there is no God, only Buddha. And Muslims say Islām is purity. We must not discard anyone, no matter what belief he holds.

We must not scorn others, because they speak a different language. People who know Arabic say that Arabic is the best language. Those who know Urdu claim that Urdu is the best,

Hindus claim that Hindi is the best, Tamil people say that Tamil is the best, and Buddhists say that Pali is the best language. The English boast that English is spoken throughout the world; the Italians say that Latin is the language of the scriptures; the Greeks say that Greek is best; the Japanese and Chinese make the same claim. There are so many different languages, and yet each person claims to be great because of the language he speaks, but greatness does not come from words.

Words are just sounds. In one language a word may have a very nice meaning, but in another language it may be obscene. Often words can cause misunderstandings that lead to fistfights and brawls.

Meaning does not lie in words themselves, meaning lies in understanding. There are so many meanings hidden within everything. There are things beyond, far beyond what we have studied up until now. We must understand this. A person who has learned several languages might think that he is a very exalted person, but he cannot speak the language that God has given to the bird. There is a story about a man who learned so much from a tiny bird that he threw away all his books.

> An *imām* named al-Ghazāli ☺ [6] had written 999 volumes about God. As he was finishing his one thousandth volume he began thinking, "I have written everything there is to write. There is nothing beyond this."
>
> One day he came to the bank of a river near the city of Rūm.[7] After unloading his books from his camel, he cooked and bathed and then began to write the final

---

6. Imām Abū Hamīd Muhammad al-Ghazāli ☺, 450-505 A.H./1058-1111 A.D.: A great Sufi who was born and died in Tus, Persia.

7. Rūm: Rome.

words of the last volume. Suddenly he saw a small bird, the size of a hummingbird, diving into the river. It flew back, perched on a twig above where Imām al-Ghazālī ☺ was writing, and dropped one or two drops of water from its tiny beak onto his book. Then it went back to the river, plunged in, flew back to its perch, and again dropped two more drops of water onto the books. Since Imām al-Ghazālī ☺ could speak the language of birds, he asked, "Oh bird, what are you doing?"

The bird replied, "I am emptying the river."

Astonished, Imām al-Ghazālī ☺ said, "Do you intend to drain the entire river? Why, you can carry only one or two drops of water at a time. At this rate, how can you ever hope to drain the entire river?"

"Of course I can," the bird answered. "And I certainly will."

"But how can you possibly do that?" Imām al-Ghazālī ☺ asked.

"Well," the little bird told him, "you have been claiming that you have reached the end of everything which can be written about Allāh. If you can reach the end of describing Allāh and His glory in a thousand books, surely I can drain this river!"

This was the wisdom that a tiny bird taught to Imām al-Ghazālī ☺. "A small bird has shown me the truth," the *imām* thought. "I have wasted all this time carrying just a drop, thinking that it was the entire river. These books must be thrown away."

So the books went into the river, and then the little bird said to him, "Since you cannot write everything about Allāh, I certainly cannot drain the river. Therefore,

I will go. *As-salāmu 'alaikum,* may the peace of God be upon you."

"*Wa 'alaikumus-salām,* may the peace of God be upon you also," the *imām* replied.

There are three or four of those books that were saved and are now circulating in the world as the works of Imām al-Ghazāli ☺. Out of the thousand books he wrote, only those few remain.

The bird in this story was really the Angel Gabriel ☺. He came to Imām al-Ghazāli ☺ to teach him wisdom, and he can also come to us in different forms to teach us. He may appear as a bird or as the wind, or even as a formless voice, or in the sounds of a child that cannot yet speak.

There are so many things we have to learn, so many hidden meanings. It is not enough just to read books. The clarity and understanding we must attain does not come from books; it is not something we can read about. To understand this we have to go beyond words, into our hearts; that is where He has revealed everything. We must dwell within Allāh and find the tongue that will reveal Him. If we have pride and say, "I have already learned a lot, I am learned," then nothing will be revealed to us. It will only happen if we grab hold of God and hold on and hold on, saying, "I surrender, I surrender, I surrender."

As soon as we accept this absolute faith and go on the straight path to God, we will realize that the good and evil in the world, the *khair* and *sharr,* are the responsibility of Allāh, His *tawakkul.* We will reject all that is *sharr,* the body and the world, and accept all that is *khair,* the eternal. When suffering comes closer and closer to us, we will embrace Allāh even more. If we live in God's embrace rather than holding onto the world, everything will be revealed to us. Instead, when we suffer we embrace the world in the way that a crab, when thrown into a fire, embraces the flames with its claws until it becomes the fire. This is the way man behaves in his ignorance.

We have to embrace that one God who is without form. That is the highest point of the *ash-shahādah kalimah*. Everything but Allāh can be destroyed; only that formless One is indestructible. That is what Islām teaches us. We must prostrate before Allāh as His *'abds,* slaves, and worship Him alone in the way that earth, fire, water, air, and ether did. We must accept our weaknesses, saying, "I am *haif.*" We must have Allāh's beautiful qualities. When these qualities of God come to bloom fragrantly within our hearts, that fragrance will comfort others and bring a state of peace which consoles all hearts. This peacefulness must come into each heart. We are all children of Adam ⊛. We came as the *Nūr* to Adam ⊛, from Allāh. When Allāh created us, He adorned us with many colors and gave us different sounds and voices. Just as a stringed instrument produces a different sound from each string according to how the musician places his fingers, God has put five strings within us, and when they are tuned and pressed in a certain way, the right resonance will come forth. Together those five strings will play, *Lā ilāha illAllāhu Muhammadur-Rasūlullāh. Ash-hādu al-lā ilāha illAllāhu wahdahu lā sharika lah; wa ash-hādu anna Muhammadan 'abduhu wa rasūluh.* There is no God but Allāh, and Muhammad is the Messenger of God. I witness that there is no God but Allāh. He is One without a partner, and I witness that Muhammad is His slave and His Messenger." If our prayer, our *dhikr,* remembrance, our meditation and worship are established in that way, they will reach God. That sound has the power to call God.

My brothers and sisters, why do we all gather together in one place when we pray? For unity. Why do we all bow our heads as one at the same time? For unity. Everywhere in the world, Muslims bow their heads as one. When we stand up, we stand up as one. When we bend, we all bend together. When we all drop to the ground in prostration at the same time, it is like saying, "We are all dead." When we rise as one, that is like saying, "Come to life." When we gather together in a Muslim house for a happy or sad occasion, we must be as one. When we attend a funeral, we recite the funeral prayer in unison to show respect for a departed brother or sister. In the name of God, we pay our respects before the corpse is buried. We do all these things in unity, because Islām is unity. In *Imān*-Islām, we must not discard anyone. We must discard only what is opposite to Allāh, only what Allāh has discarded.

Therefore, do not carry a sword, carry God's qualities. Do not carry a knife or a cannon, carry a heart of truth filled with God's beauty. Carry a compassionate face, radiant with the three thousand beautiful qualities of God. That will bring peace to others. That is Islām. Nothing in the world can conquer a heart with such qualities. Anything that tries to destroy such a heart will fail and be destroyed itself. Anything that tries to swallow something good will itself die.

We must reflect on this. We need to know how to conduct ourselves. We have to make ourselves into these qualities in order to bring them into existence. The taste of the fruit reveals the value of the tree. The fragrance and beauty of a flower show its value. The gleam from a polished gem shows the buyer its value. And we must use our lifetime to try to make ourselves valuable, to make ourselves perfectly clear. That is Islām. We can wear white clothes, but they will be white only as long as we keep them clean; how clean or dirty we are will show on our clothes. In the same way, what we think in our hearts, all the good and evil, is clearly visible to others. What is inside can be seen on the outside.

A mirror must have one side blocked off in order for us to see our reflection in the other side. Similarly, in the mirror of the *qalb*, if we block off *dunyā*, the world, on one side, we will see the light of *ākhirah*, God's kingdom, on the other. Only if we block *ākhirah*, will we see only *dunyā*.

If we block off what is evil, we will see the good, but if we block off what is good, we will see only evil. We cannot see both at the same time. Therefore, we must block off our desires and our connection to *dunyā* in order to see the side that is Islām.

Anything we look at will have a dark side and a light side, just as when the sun shines on one side of the earth, the other side is dark. One side is revealed, the other is hidden. The mind wants to look at the dark side, at *dunyā*, and if we look with the mind, then the whole world will manifest itself. If we want to look at the world, it will appear before us; that is how it takes form. If we want to look at ourselves, however, we must look into the clear side of the mirror. If we look with clear *īmān* and certitude into wisdom and God's qualities, we will see our own true image.

We have the form of man, and the light within us is a reflection that radiates from Allāh. The presence of that radiance is what we know as Islām. What we are able to see of Islām is but a reflected image; Allāh alone is Islām. Islām extends from *awwal*, the time of creation, to *ākhirah*, the next world.

This is an important introduction to the teachings of Islām, the clear teachings brought by the Rasūl ☉, the teachings of the love of Allāh. We must gently enter into this, study, and learn. However, we have to remember that we will always meet with difficulties when we try to block evil things. Any time we try to dig for something good, we will experience so much evil. There are more than four hundred trillion, ten thousand evil spiritual forces to contend with. But goodness is one—Allāh. *Āmīn. As-salāmu 'alaikum,* may the peace of God be upon you.

CHAPTER TEN

THE AFFIRMATION OF FAITH

أَشْهَدُ أَنْ لَا إِلَهَ إِلَّا اللهُ

وَحْدَهُ لَاشَرِيكَ لَهُ

وَأَشْهَدُ أَنَّ مُحَمَّدًا عَبْدُهُ وَرَسُولُهُ

Ash-Shahādah
Kalimah

The affirmation of faith

Ash-hadu al-lā ilāha illAllāhu wahdahu lā sharīka lah; wa ash-hadu anna Muhammadan 'abduhu wa rasūluh: I witness that there is nothing other than God; nothing exists; only God exists. He is One without a partner. And I witness that Muhammad is His slave and His Messenger.

Even if a rose has fifty petals, each one contains the same fragrance. Similarly, no matter how many millions of children may be in Islām, the beautiful fragrance of *kastūri,* the fragrance of Allāh's *kalimah,* will emanate from every one of them, no matter which city or country they come from, no matter what language they speak. It will be in their words, in their thoughts, in their actions, in their *īmān,* faith, in their prayers, and in their meditation.

CHAPTER TEN

THE AFFIRMATION OF FAITH

❖

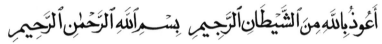

I seek refuge in Allāh from the accursed satan.
In the name of Allāh, the Most Compassionate, the Most Merciful.

Allāhu *akbar:* Allāh is most great. We are the people who have accepted Allāh; we believe in the one God and follow His Messenger, the Rasūl ☺, who brought us the holy words of the *ash-shahādah kalimah: Ash-hadu al-lā ilāha illAllāhu wahdahu lā sharika lah; wa ash-hādu anna Muhammadan 'abduhu wa rasūluh. Lā ilāha illAllāh Muhammadur-Rasūlullāh:* I witness that there is no God but Allāh. He is One without a partner, and I witness that Muhammad is His slave and His Messenger. Other than God nothing exists. Only You are God, and Muhammad is His Messenger.[1]

Let us speak about the *ash-shahādah kalimah* sent down by Allāh to the Rasūl ☺. For whom are these words meant? We need to reflect on this. The Rasūl ☺ was born in Mecca into the Quraish[2] tribe. Does that mean that the *kalimah* is meant only for

---

1. See Appendix: Five *Kalimahs.*

2. Quraish: The Arabian tribe from which Muhammad ☺ was descended and of which his grandfather, 'Abdul-Muttalib, was chief.

141

the Quraish? No, it has spread to all the different tribes throughout Africa and the Middle East and to people the world over, of
every race and religion. Look how many Muslims there are in the
world today.

Who has the right to call himself a Muslim and who does not?
To whom does Islām belong? Does it belong to one sect more
than to another? A person might say he follows one of the four
imāms: Imām Abū Hanīfah, Imām Mālik, Imām ibn Hanbal, and
Imām ash-Shāfi'ī,[3] but does it really matter to which family or
tribe or sect he belongs, or whether he is an Arab or not? Anyone,
anywhere, who has said the *ash-shahādah kalimah* is in Islām. It
is our duty to recite that *kalimah* with *īmān,* absolute faith and
perfect certitude. One who does this is a Muslim and a *mu'min,*
true believer, and he dwells within Islām.

We become Muslims and *mu'mins* by accepting the *kalimah*
and by becoming the followers of the Final Prophet, Muhammad
Mustāfār Rasūl ☻, the Prophet for the beginning and for the end.
Everything that was given in the beginning was made complete in
him. By accepting this Truth and the one Treasure called Allāh,
we can receive the wealth of the three worlds, the *mubārakāt* of
Allāh's *rahmah,* grace.

Allāh belongs equally to everyone. Every tongue that has
recited the *ash-shahādah kalimah* belongs to the same family and

---

3. Imām Abū Hanīfah ☻: Born in al-Kūfah and died in Baghdad. 80-150 A.H./700-
767 A.D.
   Imām Mālik ☻: Born and died in Medina. 94-179 A.H./716-795 A.D.
   Imām ibn Hanbal ☻: Born and died in Baghdad. 164-241 A.H./780-855 A.D.
   Imām ash-Shāfi'ī ☻: Born in Askalon, Palestine and died in Cairo. 150-
204 A.H./767-820 A.D.
   These four men systematically developed the rules of conduct and law, *fiqh,*
from the injunctions appearing in the Qur'ān and the *hadīth.* Four different
schools of thought were established after them, each having a slightly different
interpretation of the practices of Islām.

is part of the same body of true believers. They are all children born to one mother. This is unity, this is oneness. To believe in Islām with *īmān* is to live in that one body.

Therefore, anyone who has truly accepted the Prophet ☺ and has faith in the *kalimah* will never harm or kill another who has also affirmed these words no matter what fault that person may have committed. A tongue that has recited the *kalimah,* a tongue that has accepted Allāh and the Rasūl ☺, should never attack another person in any way.

By reciting the *ash-shahādah kalimah,* it is possible for us to attain a certain state, but we must remember that those who have not recited the *kalimah,* affirmation of faith, are still our neighbors. We must love them, not destroy them. Neighbors are not there to fight with, they are not there to be our enemies. Once we have recited the *kalimah,* we must show others only love, trust, and friendship. We must melt our neighbors' hearts and make them trust us and embrace us. Then they will begin to act in the same way themselves.

Islām does not mean killing or attacking others. When such a thing happens, Islām is harming itself. To embrace others with love and to dispel their hunger, disease, poverty, and difficulties is Islām. To speak to someone from within the embrace of unity is Islām. To be together, to eat together, to live as one life in a state of affection is Islām. That is love, God's love, and Islām is the affection shown through that love. Islām is the compassion shown by acting with God's three thousand gracious qualities. Islām is establishing the praise of God and establishing the qualities of *sabūr,* inner patience, *shukūr,* contentment, *tawakkul,* surrendering all responsibility to God, and *al-hamdu lillāh,* praising God for whatever happens. Islām is Allāhu *akbar:* the one God is most great. One who is in Islām will practice these good qualities and continually beg of God, "*Astaghfirullāhal-'aliyyal-'azīm:* O Allāh, forgive all our faults and correct us." That is what it means to be a *mu'min,* to be in Islām.

To become one is Islām. Just as five fingers come together to form one hand, to be one with every group is Islām. There is only one group in Islām, the group which loves Allāh, the group of Muhammad ⊕. There are seventy-three different groups of human beings, but out of those, Islām is the one that has faith in God without the slightest doubt or wavering.

There is only one race for a Muslim; there is no black, white, or yellow. There is no fighting and no division. How can we divide Islām and fight over it? How can we listen to people who goad us into fighting by complaining, "Those men are different from us." The nature of true Islām is to bring together what has been divided. Once we were separate and divided and scattered in many different directions, but the *kalimah* and Islām brought us together to worship the one God and embrace each other heart to heart.

We must be one. We must not create divisions by talk of different people, different positions, or different status. There are no divisions within Islām. Once someone has said the *ash-shahādah kalimah* there is only one way to describe him: a child of Islām. Nothing else. Earlier he might have been different, but now he is a Muslim. He might have been in another religion before, but now he is in Islām.

True Islām is unity. There are no titles and no differences. There is only one great title: *Yā* Allāh, *Yā Maulā.* We may call men of wisdom by the title of *maulā,* and we may even call those who have converted to Islām *maulal-*Islām, but Allāh alone is the *Maulā,* the Lord, the Master in Islām. We have to become slaves to Him alone. He is the only One worthy of worship.

We must not create divisions in Islām by calling some high and others low. There is no such thing in the *kalimah.* Can we recite the *kalimah* and then separate Muslims into different categories, saying some are high and some are low? No, we cannot say that. A tree may have many branches, but the flowers and fruits on that tree are all the same. Is that not so? What does it matter if a fruit is on a lower branch or a higher one? Their seeds are the same.

We cannot show favoritism in Islām. We are all the creations of Allāh, the children of Adam ☺, the tribe of Abraham ☺, the followers of Muhammad ☺. He sends food to all and protects us all. Tomorrow He will question us all, no matter who we are or what position we hold. On the Day of *Qiyāmah,* Questioning, judgment will be given for the good and evil each of us has gathered. Before that time we cannot tell if someone is good or bad, or high or low in status. We are all Adam's ☺ children, all fruits from the same tree.

Of course, there is one small difference. Some fruits may be fully ripe and very tasty, some may be in the process of ripening, and some may still be as hard as rock. But we cannot hurry the unripe fruits by beating them. Each one will ripen in its own time, according to how much sun it receives and whether the wind blows on it from a southerly or northerly direction. Similarly, if we want to help the children of Adam ☺ to ripen, we can only do it by showering them with good qualities, not by beating them. We have to ripen them and make them peaceful with the kind of loving affection that regards other lives as our own.

We have been told, "Love your neighbor as you love yourself." We have not been told to beat our neighbor, to kill him, or to cut him up. That will not ripen him. Only if a man's heart is melting with love can he reach a state of acceptance. His heart has to be right. When we show someone love, compassion, trust, and friendship, he will melt in our embrace. Affection evokes affection. Let us embrace our neighbors as the Rasūl ☺ has taught us. Let us share with them the things that Allāh has given us. To live together in unity with all groups is the proof that we are all the children of Adam ☺. Love your neighbor as yourself; do not take his land and kill him.

You must not accumulate wealth and destroy your good qualities. Money is a dead body, a corpse. *Imān* is your only wealth. *Imān* is your paradise, your *firdaus*. Only truth and goodness will stay with you when you die. You cannot hold onto anything else. You cannot divide up the earth and keep a share for yourself. Anything taken from the earth will have to be given back to it. Nor can you divide up the water and keep a portion as your own. You can drink a thousand cups of water, but you have to eliminate it sometimes. You cannot hold on to water. No matter how much you take, earth belongs to earth and water belongs to water.

The Rasūl ☺ gave us the laws and the words of God, but he did not seek to hold on to wealth or land or possessions in exchange. He did not want such things. All he wanted was for us to accept Allāh. How did he get us to do that? By showing us good qualities. He gave us the *kalimah* and the wealth of his qualities. He told us, "This is your true wealth; this is what will help you. Take it and share it with others." The Rasūl ☺ taught us to love our neighbors, to let them follow any religion they wanted to, and to be free to worship any god they chose. If our neighbors wish to come to pray with us, then we must let them come. We should never attack them. Instead, we should live with them in unity and love and be happy together.

The Rasūl ☺ also taught us that one who is in Islām must never attack another who is in Islām. If there is fighting even among those who have declared the *kalimah,* think how much worse it could be among people who have not. When one person who has affirmed these words attacks another who has, that cannot be called Islām. Anyone who has said the *kalimah* is your own flesh, for you are made from the *sūrah,* form, of the *kalimah.* You are one family, the creations of Allāh, whom His Light has touched. This is the absolute truth. It is the hidden treasure that was brought by the Rasūl ☺.

Islām will become one only when Muslims think like this, when they accept this oneness and act accordingly. Only then will Islām progress and this treasure grow. But when one Muslim attacks another, when one Muslim acts treacherously towards another, when a Muslim takes revenge against his neighbors or kills them, such acts hasten the destruction of the world. Should that happen and evil ways prevail, then truth, *īmān,* faith, the *mubārakāt,* wealth of the three worlds, and the *Qudrah,* Power, of the *Rahmatul-'ālamīn,* the Grace of all the universes, will fail to benefit us; they will be wasted.

A Muslim must reflect upon the true meaning of Islām and the meaning within the divine words of the Holy Qur'ān. People quote the Qur'ān constantly, but is that enough? Some people can memorize the thirty *juz',* sections, of the Qur'ān in two or three years. Is that all that must be done? The Qur'ān does not consist only of the words we memorize; there are countless points and explanations contained within those words.

We need to understand every single point behind the words we read; we need to understand the meaning of every single thing we do. For example, let us look at the inner meaning of *qurbān,* the ritual slaughter of animals. Before the time of Muhammad ☺, people could slaughter a chicken, a goat, a cow, a camel, or any other animal whenever they wanted to. They could just pick up a chicken and wring its neck. Islām put a stop to this. Instead of allowing slaughter in every house at random, the people were asked to come to the mosque to have the *lebbe,* one who does duty in the mosque, slaughter the animals in the way that was *halāl,* permissible, according to the laws of *qurbān.*

Some people came and complained to the Rasūl ☺, saying, "My children are going without food. We waited for the *lebbe* to do the *qurbān,* but he had to go to prayers and do other things, so there was not enough time for him to slaughter our animals."

Muhammad ☺ then said, "Instead of a hundred chickens, slaughter two goats. Instead of a hundred goats, slaughter ten cows. Instead of ten cows, slaughter three or four camels. Then, if you share the meat fairly, according to the size of each family, everyone will get what they need." Little by little, the Rasūl ☺ told them these things, in order to reduce the killing in the country. Since they had to observe these strict limits, only five to ten animals a day could be slaughtered instead of thousands. They could not kill as they pleased; they could take only what they needed.

The *hadīth* also tell of the Rasūl ☺ saying to 'Alī ☺, "Meat is one of the few foods available in our country, but if you eat the meat of an animal for forty days in a row, the qualities of that animal will come into you. Never eat meat for forty days in a row, 'Alī. We should reduce our consumption of meat."

Why were these laws made? To stop the random killing of animals. If the Rasūl ☺ tried to reduce even the slaughter of animals, should we increase the slaughter of men? How can those within a brotherhood attack and kill each other? If one person even gossips about another, and that person then gossips about the first in retaliation, fighting and death will result on all sides.

There was fighting before the Rasūl ☺ brought the *kalimah,* but there is no excuse for it now. Now our neighbor is our brother, whether he recites the *kalimah* or not. We must trust him and he must trust us. We are in Islām, and that means we are in unity. The true meaning of Islām is to embrace our neighbors and love them as we love ourselves. Each of us must think about this and look deeply into our hearts. We must pay careful attention to all of Allāh's words. We must examine the inner secrets of the words of the Qur'ān and the meanings of every *hadīth*, every word the Rasūl ☻ has spoken. We must understand every meaning within the *kalimah* and embrace each other in unity. If we can exist in that state, we will be in Islām. That is unshakable Islām, the great treasure given by the *Rahmatul-'ālamīn* to those of us who have received the *mubārakāt,* the wealth of the three worlds. When that wealth is ours, we will see peace, harmony, and unity. That is success. May we reflect upon this.

We must always think: What is Islām? Islām is like a rose. Even if a rose has fifty petals, each one contains the same fragrance. Similarly, no matter how many millions of children may be in Islām, the beautiful fragrance of *kastūrī,*[4] the fragrance of Allāh's *kalimah,* will emanate from every one of them, no matter which city or country they come from, no matter what language they speak. It will be in their words, in their thoughts, in their actions, in their *īmān,* faith, in their prayers, and in their meditation. It will be in their *kalimah,* in their *toluhai,* ritual prayer, in their *'ibādah,* devotion, in their *dhikr,* remembrance, and in their *fikr,* deep concentration on God. That fragrance is there in the petals of every *qalb.* We must try to know that fragrance.

The blood that unites us as one is the *kalimah.* As followers of the Rasūl ☻, we must be one. That is the meaning of Islām. That

---

4. *kastūrī* (T) The fragrance of the beautiful qualities of Allāh. Literally, a musk fragrance.

is what it means to be a *mu'min*, true believer. If we can establish a state of unity and trust, Islām can never again descend to the state it has come to now. Today practically every Islamic country is at war with another. Wherever we look we see divisions, separations, and wars. That is not Islām.

To wage war within oneself is Islām; the real fight is an inner one. To dispel evil qualities, evil thoughts, and the differences that lead to separations is Islām. To wage war upon jealousy, envy, and vengeance is Islām. To cut out and discard the qualities of satan and to fill ourselves with the qualities of Allāh is Islām. To show a heart full of love to our brothers and sisters is the wealth of Islām.

We must embrace each brother and sister with love and trust. We have to think of each one of God's qualities and fill ourselves with them, one by one, little by little. That is true love. There should not be one trace of prejudice in us. There should not be any words within us that are different from the words we speak outwardly.

The words of *īmān* and Islām are like rays of light emerging from the sun. No matter how many clouds cover the sun, it will emerge from behind them and shine again. The clouds cannot change the sun. In the same way, the clouds of karma, sin, and satan, and the evil clouds of jealousy and revenge will come and try to conceal our light. But when faith, certitude, and determination stand firm, they will push those clouds away, and the radiant light of truth will once again shine forth from us.

To always shine with the beautiful light and form of *īmān*, absolute faith, is Islām. And to become sweeter as we think of this is Islām. If we understand God's qualities, we will find them sweet. If we act with God's actions, they will be sweet. When we embrace our brothers and sisters with those actions and with trust, we will realize what happiness is and know the goodness that comes from it. As we embrace each brother and sister heart to heart, helping them in whatever way they need, we will know what joy and goodness are.

As children of Adam ☻, as members of the tribe of Abraham ☻, as the followers of Muhammad ☻ and the disciples of Allāh, we must understand this. Islām is to join together as one, knowing that those who have not affirmed the *kalimah* are our neighbors and that those who have affirmed the *kalimah* are intermingled within our own bodies.

This is the most important aspect of Islām: oneness. The tongue which says the *kalimah* makes us one. This tongue has to protect Islām. To protect our neighbors from danger is Islām. First we must see that we ourselves do not kill them, and then we must embrace them. We must act according to the laws that have been sent down. Every word in our hearts must follow those laws; we must not go beyond them. The words of Allāh, the words of the Rasūl ☻ and the Qur'ān, the words of truth, conscience, integrity, and of justice are law.

For a human being there are four kinds of justice: God's justice, the king's justice, man's justice, and the justice of each conscience. First we must act with God's justice. Then we must become the king inside our bodies, controlling ourselves and ruling justly over the four hundred trillion, ten thousand spiritual qualities and the millions of actions that are there within us. We must then become that king's subjects, acting with justice towards all mankind. Finally, justice becomes the inner witness, the conscience, and we can begin to live as human beings, complete in the state of justice.

We must reflect on this. Only then can we understand what true Islām is and know who we are. If we live in such a state, these qualities will spread, the *kalimah* will spread, and love, trust, and friendship will spread.

Therefore, embrace every heart and make everyone your brother. Send forth from yourself the quality of embracing others and let that love touch and touch and touch their hearts, making them peaceful. That is Islām. Do not send a sword, a knife, a hatchet, or a bomb. Send the *kalimah,* send the words of the Rasūl ☉, send Allāh's three thousand gracious qualities and His ninety-nine *wilāyats.* Send love forth from your heart to others.

If you embrace people in this way, you will realize so much happiness and sweetness, as heart after heart after heart is captured. It will turn them into exalted beings, beings of peace and tranquility. It will turn them into *gnānis,* men of wisdom, virtuous beings with compassionate hearts. We must bring God's qualities into our actions and make them a part of us. We are told to feed the hungry and to give *sadaqah,* charity, to others. Giving money is not enough; embracing others and giving them good qualities is a much greater charity. Giving wisdom is an even greater charity, and to have *īmān* and become a brother is the greatest charity of all. Then you will truly eat from one plate, not two. Two is not true *sadaqah.*

Precious children, jeweled lights of my eyes, my brothers and sisters, every one of us must reflect on this and do it without fail. It must come into our understanding and live within our hearts. We must know it in our worship. It must resplend from within our inner beings and emerge from our lives as a treasure.

Islām is the greatest blessing we can receive. All that we can ever understand in life is within Islām. When we are buried and questioned in the grave and the verdict is given, it is all within Islām. It is all one. The treasures of Islām that we receive are treasures of Allāh's *rahmah,* grace, treasures of His *mubārakāt.*

The words I have just spoken came from my heart. They came in the name of Allāh and the Rasūl ☉. They came from the *qalb*, from the innermost heart of one who has not learned anything. I am a *miskīn*, just a poor man. I have not studied. Every word came from my heart. If there is any fault in what I have said, please forgive me. Every brother and sister, I most humbly beg you to forgive me in the name of Allāh and the Rasūl ☉.

Āmīn. As-salāmu 'alaikum wa rahmatullāhi wa barakātuhu kulluhu. So be it. May all the peace, the beneficence, and the blessings of God be upon you.

THE OCEAN OF DIVINE KNOWLEDGE

Al-'Ilm

Divine knowledge

You are the Qur'ān; you are your own book. If you can study that book and reach the state of fully-ripened 'ilm, you will be able to speak of its sweetness and know peace and comfort in your life. To establish and understand this state is Īmān-Islām. To learn 'ilm is Islām. Once we understand this, we will understand why the Rasūl ⊕ said, "Study 'ilm, even if you have to go unto China."

CHAPTER ELEVEN

THE OCEAN OF DIVINE KNOWLEDGE

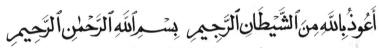

أَعُوذُ بِاللَّهِ مِنَ الشَّيْطَانِ الرَّجِيمِ بِسْمِ اللَّهِ الرَّحْمَنِ الرَّحِيمِ

I seek refuge in Allāh from the accursed satan.
In the name of Allāh, the Most Compassionate, the Most Merciful.

This is a small explanation of *Īmān*-Islām, the way the Sufis practice it as they develop more and more clarity and wisdom.

Throughout the ages, step-by-step, Allāh sent revelations to mankind through the prophets—through Adam, Noah, Abraham, Ishmael, Moses, David, Jesus, and through all the other prophets, may the peace of God be upon them. One prophet brought ten revelations, another brought seven, and others came with only one, two, or three. The *kalimah* was also given to the prophets, each receiving it in a slightly different form.

As His final and ultimate explanation Allāh sent 6,666 revelations to the Final Prophet, Muhammad ☺, who was also the Prophet for the beginning, *Nūr Muhammad*. Those revelations are the *āyats*, verses, of the Qur'ān, and they include all the revelations sent to earlier prophets. We were provided with these explanations so that we could understand the words, conduct, and qualities of *Īmān*-Islām, and the value of the *kalimah*.

Allāh has given us five *kalimahs*[1] and ordained five times of prayer each day. These are essential for our peace and contentment. Earth, fire, water, air, and ether are also five in number and are necessary for the life of the body. All creations suffer when their bodies are deprived of water, when they do not have enough air to breathe, or when they feel the fire of hunger. If it is too hot the body needs something cooling, if it becomes cold the body must have heat. Only after these needs are satisfied can the body feel peaceful. Similarly, only when we receive a full understanding of *Īmān*-Islām and the *ash-shahādah kalimah* can we realize the extent of the peace they offer.

God has provided all that we require to meet our inner and outer needs, at every moment, wherever we are. But in order to know exactly what will comfort us and what will quench our thirst, we have to know everything in *awwal, dunyā,* and *ākhirah,* the time of creation, this world, and the hereafter. So that we can understand all this, Allāhu ta'ālā has given the Qur'ān.

The Qur'ān is an ocean of divine knowledge, the *bahrul-'ilm.* It is so vast that its breadth can never be seen and its depth can never be fathomed. To try to limit it thinking, "That's all there is to it," is ignorant. That ocean contains everything: heaven, hell, this world, and the eighteen thousand universes. We have been told, "Swim! Immerse yourself in that ocean of *'ilm.*" If we want to know the secrets and the stories it contains, we must obtain the strength of wisdom to dive deep within it and deep into the qualities of God. We must cling to the faith that the *kalimah* inspires as we repeat its words and swim with the power of the *kalimah's* radiance.

To cross this ocean of *'ilm* each one of us must become an

---

1. Five *Kalimahs:* See Appendix.

insān kāmil, a perfected human being. Such a person lives his life with wisdom, and when he swims, he knows. But in our present state we seem to be floating on this endless ocean, tied to a flimsy raft. With certitude we must hold fast to the oar of faith in Allāh and the Rasūl ☺, knowing that Allāh is the upper edge and the Rasūl ☺ is the lower edge of the blade which moves through the water pushing us forward. Then we can cross the ocean and reach the shore.

My brothers and sisters, if you can know your own life and understand it, you will find that vast ocean within you. You will find the Qur'ān within you. You are the Qur'ān; you are your own book. If you can study that book and reach the state of fully-ripened *'ilm,* you will be able to speak of its sweetness and know peace and comfort in your life. To establish and understand this state is *Īmān*-Islām. To learn *'ilm* is Islām. Once we understand this, we will understand why the Rasūl ☺ said, "Study *'ilm,* even if you have to go unto China."

Wherever we are, *'ilm* will bring us the right thing at the right time. As we mature step-by-step, the right thing will become known to us. This is how we must delve within the Qur'ān. To try to understand the Qur'ān through tricks of the intellect will not work. Nor can we receive its benefits by earning the titles and esteem of the world. These things belong to satan. To try to see the value of the Qur'ān with the mind is useless. The mind cannot grasp divine knowledge. We can only understand *'ilm* if we surrender to God and have perfect trust in Him, knowing that He is the One who can do all things. We must study *'ilm* through the clarity of pure wisdom, with a pure soul, and through the pure qualities of *sabūr,* inner patience, *shukūr,* contentment, *tawakkul,* trust in God, *al-hamdu lillāh,* praise of God, and the acknowledgement that God is most great and can do all things.

God's beautiful qualities, duties, and actions are Islām. He is each quality, He is each duty, He is each action. He performs His duties and actions with His qualities. He is what He does. He acts, He sees, He questions, He gives, He receives. These are the meanings of His ninety-nine names, the *asmā'ul-husnā*. These *wilāyats*, powers, of Allāh can be found in the *qalb* of each and every human being as qualities, actions, and behavior. They are the highest ideals of Islām, and they must be developed and established. Man must invite them into his heart.

When these ninety-nine *wilāyats* of Allāh, His three thousand divine attributes, the qualities of the Rasūlullāh ☺, and the *salām*, the *salawāt*, and the *kalimah* begin to resonate within the heart of a man, he will not have any enemies. When *sabūr, shukūr, tawakkul, al-hamdu lillāh,* and Allāhu *akbar* resplend within him, his *qalb* will resonate with the qualities of unity, humility, and harmony. He will have no prejudices or differences. When the *dhikr,* the remembrance of God, and *fikr,* contemplation on God, begin to resonate in his *qalb,* that resonance will bring millions and millions of explanations that will bring peace to millions of hearts. Such a person will care for his neighbor as himself. He will have the ability to hold everyone in an embrace which makes them all one. He will never see anyone as an enemy, because Allāh has no enemy.

Allāh is each one of His names. Not one of His names has the meaning of attacking or causing pain. It is not God's work to attack others; His work is to correct what comes to Him. If something is wrong, He corrects it with His wisdom. What Allāh does is Islām. In the same way, one who is in Islām will correct his own faults in order to bring peace to others. He will correct his own qualities in order to soothe and comfort others. He will teach God's qualities to his mind and elevate his own state to the state of God so that he can help others to grow.

When every heart understands this, when these qualities develop in the heart of one human being and then transfer to the hearts of other human beings, when unity and love catch every heart, every life, and every nation, then true Islām will come into being and catch fire and spread throughout the world. He will have the ability to hold everyone in an embrace which makes them all one. Allāh has no hostility; and the *kalimah* the Rasūl ☉ brought expresses no hostility. Once we say that *kalimah*, and accept the truth of God with absolute faith, we will accept everyone and everything as Islām. Drawing a sword, attacking others, or trying to force them into our beliefs is not Islām. Controlling yourself, controlling the anger, jealousy, and vengeance that come from your own mind, and attacking all the thoughts within us that hurt others is the true meaning of Islām. That is the war we all must wage.

God has no need to wage wars. He is capable of creating or destroying universes within the blink of an eye. If He were to close His eye, nothing would exist; if He opened it again creation would come back to life. In the blink of an eye, the darkness within the *qalb*, the inner heart, can be dispelled and the light of God's qualities can come to life.

Is-lām. Lām is light, the pure soul and the pure wisdom. The word Islām describes a place where there is no darkness at all, a place where there are no differences, no disputes over races or religions, a place where there is only light. As we open our eyes and our hearts to that light, to inner patience, and to the wisdom of *'ilm,* all our evil tendencies will be burned away, and all of God's beauty will come into being within us. Of course, if we do not recognize the difference between good and evil, we might burn everything indiscriminately. But if we apply our understanding we will burn away only the bad. Then light will come into being, and we will see the power of God's grace and understand what Islām truly is. One who understands this will gain the wealth, the *mubārakāt*, of the three worlds. For such a man, this world known as *dunyā* is heaven, the hereafter is heaven, and even *awwal*, the time of creation, of birth, is heaven.

Īmān-Islām is the name given to this state when it is established with awareness. But as long as we do not understand this properly and continue to say, "I am great, I am greater than you," we have not reached that level of understanding. Only when we have rid ourselves of all our blemishes will we be able to see God.

My brothers and sisters, even though we have not yet seen God, there is no place where He does not exist. He is within every life. He is in the trees, the flowers, the fruits, and in the plants and shrubs and vines. There would be no flowers or fruits on a tree if His Power did not exist within it. When we squeeze a fruit, its sweet juice can quench our thirst and satisfy our hunger, because it has His Power within it.

The same intensity of sweetness is in Islām, in the ideals of Islām. When we accept the qualities of Allāh and the Rasūl ☻, when we recite the *kalimah*, the *salām*, greeting of peace, and the *salawāt*, prayers, we will experience that sweetness. The trust inspired by that love will melt our hearts and touch the hearts of everyone around us. We will be like honeybees collecting the honey of Islām from a million flowers and storing it within our heart. Islām is the honey that unites, the honey that we can taste and enjoy and share with everyone else. We are filled with God's beautiful qualities and actions; we will embrace all lives as our own in unity. Our racial and religious prejudices will leave us. Doubt, jealousy, and the spilling of blood will cease. As long as we do not reach that state of *'ilm* and wisdom and clarity, trouble will arise. Only when the qualities of *Īmān*-Islām come into us will we see Islām in everyone.

All of creation is within Islām. God created everything and everyone as Islām, as light. Who is not in Islām? Everything is contained within Islām. Since the time of Adam ☺ everything has been in Islām. Adam, Noah, Abraham, Ishmael, Moses, David, and Jesus, may the peace of God be upon them, and Muhammad ☺ are all within Islām. Idris, Isaac, Job, Jacob, Sālih, and the many other prophets, may the peace of God be upon them all, are also within Islām. Everyone created is within Islām. God never called anyone anything else. It is we who call ourselves by different races and different tribes. Such arrogance causes destruction. It destroys us and it destroys others. We end up fighting each other and hurting each other. Wisdom means not hurting anyone. With *sabūr*, patience, we should embrace one another. And when our difficulties increase, we must continue to embrace each other and have *shukūr*, contentment. When problems get even worse, the sweetness of our embrace must deepen and we must have *tawakkul*, surrender to Allāh, and say, "*Al-hamdu lillāh*, all praise is to You. I have done as much as I can, it is Your responsibility now. *Al-hamdu lillāh*. I praise You!" If the situation becomes impossible we say, "Allāhu *akbar*, You are the greatest, I die within You. Accept me." Those qualities are the honey, the taste, and the fruit of Islām. Through them you can reach the highest level of *Īmān*-Islām and find the contentment you need in your life. Then you will be able to comfort others and help them find the treasure of peace that the world is lacking.

My love you. May God help us. *As-salāmu 'alaikum*. May the peace of God be with you.

CHAPTER TWELVE

THE INNER QUR'ĀN

Ummul-Qur'ān

The mother or source of the Qur'ān

Allāh and the state of an *insān* are right here within us. It is a great secret, hidden within our *qalbs*, inner hearts, within the *Ummul*-Qur'ān. Only if we can study this *'ilm*, divine knowledge, can we attain our freedom.

THE INNER QUR'ĀN

I seek refuge in Allāh from the accursed satan.
In the name of Allāh, the Most Compassionate, the Most Merciful.

*B*ismillāhir-Rahmānir-Rahīm. In the name of God, the Most Compassionate, the Most Merciful. *As-salāmu 'alaikum wa rahmatullāhi wa barakātuhu kulluhu.* May all the peace, the beneficence, and the blessings of God be upon you.

Brothers and sisters in Islām, the Qur'ān is a vast ocean of divine knowledge, a *bahrul-'ilm*. No matter what changes occur throughout the ages, the Qur'ān is one thing that never changes. It is immutable. It offers an explanation appropriate for every period of time and for every level of understanding. All the meanings it contains could not be written down even if all the oceans of the world were made into ink and all the trees were made into pens.

To comprehend the Qur'ān, first we must establish our *īmān*, our absolute faith, certitude, and determination; then we must acquire wisdom; and finally we must delve deep inside and study it from within. If we look into the depths of the Qur'ān, we will find the complete *rahmah*, the never-ending wealth of Allāhu ta'ālā's grace. We will find the Light of Allāh, the Resplendence of Allāh. We will not find racial or religious prejudices, battles, or fighting of any kind. We will find only the benevolence of all the universes, the *Rahmatul-'ālamīn*.

The Qur'ān appeared as *Awwal Muhammad* (the beginning, the emergence of creation), as *Hayāt Muhammad* (the eternal life, the emergence of the soul), as *An'am Muhammad* (the food, the *rizq*, the nourishment for all creations), as *Ahmad* (the heart, the *qalb*), as *Muhammad* (the beauty of the face which is a reflection of the beauty of the heart), and as *Nūr Muhammad* (the plenitude, the Light which became completeness within Allāh and then emerged).

The Qur'ān is a treasure which continually speaks to our *īmān*, to our faith. Its verses were sent to the Rasūlullāh ⊕ one by one, according to the needs of the people, the difficulties they were undergoing at that time, and the questions they asked. These *āyats*, verses, and *sūrats*, chapters, were sent to bring clarity to *insān*, man, from the time he appears as the *mīm*,[1] as a fetus, to the moment he reaches the shore of *ākhirah*, the hereafter. They cleanse man stage by stage. Whatever state he is in at one *waqt*, time of prayer, the Qur'ān explains the state he should achieve by the next *waqt*. In this way, the Qur'ān lifts man up, causing his wisdom, his beauty, and his *'ilm*, divine knowledge, to grow little by little.

The Rasūlullāh ⊕ said, "Even though I depart from the world, I leave you the Qur'ān. That is your evidence. Please keep it close to you. The Qur'ān will be a shaikh, teacher, and a *sayyid*, learned one, to each *qalb*, inner heart." That is why its *āyats* were sent to mankind. Verse by verse, the Qur'ān cuts away all the things

---

1. *mīm* (A) The Arabic letter which correlates to the English consonant "m." Its shape is similar to the sperm cell.

within man that need to be discarded, and step by step it elevates him.

That is the purpose of the Qur'ān—to eliminate man's four hundred trillion, ten thousand degenerate qualities and actions which oppose the truth of God, and to show man how to develop, how to beautify and improve himself. It has the capacity to cut away this birth, arrogance, karma, maya, and the energies of *tārahan, singhan,* and *sūran,* the three sons of maya. It can dispel man's love for earth, woman, and gold. It can drive away desire, anger, miserliness, attachment, bigotry, envy, intoxication, lust, theft, murder, and falsehood.

To rid himself of these evil qualities, an *insān,* human being, must sacrifice and purify his *qalb* for Allāh. He must perform this *qurbān*[2] for the sake of truth and justice, for the sake of righteous action, duty, equality, peacefulness, unity, and for the love of the one human family. If he does this, he will acquire the qualities, actions, and beauty of Allāh. This is the state which the Qur'ān depicts, the state of *dīnul*-Islām, the path of perfect purity. This is Allāh's kingdom, and He is the only One who protects it, conducts its affairs, and rules over it with total justice. Anyone who acts according to that justice and understands Allāh in completeness becomes His *'abd,* slave. Such a man possesses nothing of his own, and so Allāh protects him and looks after all his needs.

If a man progresses to this state of purity, if he succeeds in performing this *qurbān,* in cutting away all these evil qualities, then he becomes a *mu'min,* a true believer, living for nothing other than Allāh, and having nothing other than Allāh in his thoughts or intentions. He does not concern himself with seeing or hearing

---

2. *qurbān* (A) Externally, it is the ritual slaughter of animals to make them permissible to eat. Inwardly, it is to sacrifice one's life in devotion to God and to cut away the beastly qualities within the heart of man.

others, because no one else exists for him. He sees nothing other than Allāh. He speaks to no one other than Allāh. He has closed himself off to the sight and sound of everything but Allāh. That is why he is called an *ummī,* an unlettered one. Because he has no words of his own, Allāh's words and sounds come through him. He becomes the *hadīth,* which explains the inner and outer aspects of Allāh's revelations. In that state his *sūrah,* body or form, is the *kitāb,* the holy book, and his *qalb* is the *Ummul-Qur'ān.* What does *ummul* mean? It means mother. The mother who raises the *mu'min,* true believer, is the *Ummul-*Qur'ān, the mother of justice and *īmān,* the mother of *insān's* wisdom and his faith. The *Ummul-*Qur'ān is the essence of the Qur'ān, the eye of the Qur'ān. If *insān* will open that eye, he will know Allāh, and knowing Allāh, he will hear only His sounds and His words. This was the state of the Rasūlullāh, *Ummī Muhammad* ⊕. The Rasūlullāh ⊕ was unlearned, and therefore, the words that he received could only have come through God's revelation, *wahy.* Allāh explained to Muhammad ⊕ the meaning of everything He had revealed to the earlier prophets. He explained *Īmān*-Islām, *salāh,* prayer, and *'ibādah,* worship. And it was through this Final Prophet that Allāh clarified everything to mankind.

Of all the prophets, only Moses ⊕ and Muhammad ⊕ attained the state where they met and spoke directly to God—Moses ⊕ on Mount Sinai, when God revealed Himself as a resplendent Light, and Muhammad ⊕ on several occasions, once face to face during *mi'rāj,* his mystical journey to heaven, and also in the many direct revelations, *hadīth qudsī.*

Moses ⊕ and Muhammad ⊕ also shared another distinction. They were the only two prophets whose names began with the letter *mīm* (or "m"). The *mīm* was what Allāh created first, and from it He made all of His creations. Through that *mīm* Allāh

gave Moses ☺ the Ten Commandments and the explanations of
the Torah, showing him what was *halāl* and *harām*, permissible
and forbidden according to God's law, and what was *khair* and
sharr, good and evil. With the grace of that *mīm*, Moses ☺ was
able to perform miracles and to deliver his people from Pharoah.
And it was to the *mīm* in Muhammad ☺ that Allāh revealed the
6,666 *āyats* of the Qur'ān.

The letter *mīm* covers the universes of *awwal*, *dunyā*, and
ākhirah, the stage of creation, this world, and the hereafter. It pen-
etrates the *dhāt* and *sifāt*, the essence and manifestation, as well
as *khair* and *sharr*, good and evil. All creations begin with *mīm*,
the pearl of creation. As long as creations continue to appear, that
mīm will exist. It is endless. The Sufis say that it is impossible to
give a complete explanation of the *mīm*; it can only be grasped by
those who search deeply with perfect *īmān* and an open *qalb*.

How then is it possible to explain who Muhammad ☺ truly
is? How can we say when Muhammad ☺ was created or when
he appeared? Only if we understand the real Qur'ān completely
can we understand Muhammad ☺. The Sufis also say that only
when man comes to a realization of himself and dives deep within the Qur'ān, drinking from its inner essence, will the truth of
Muhammad ☺ be revealed to him in meditation. Until he reaches that state, he will continue to say that Muhammad ☺ is the
son of Āminah ☺ and 'Abdullāh ☺. The Sufis call Muhammad ☺
the Light of the *qalb*, the inner heart. In Tamil *muham* means
face and *aham* means heart. When the *ahmad*, the state of the
heart, becomes Muhammad ☺, then the light of the inner heart
is revealed as the beauty of the face. That is the *dīn*, the essence,
of Islam.

Those who follow the Prophet Muhammad-Mustāfār-Rasūl ☺
and have the perfect clarity of *īmān*, absolute faith, certitude,

and determination, are known as Muslims. For those who have accepted the *īmān* of Islām, Allāh has decreed five outer *furūd,* duties, and six inner *furūd.*

The first outer *fard,* obligatory duty, for those who have perfect *īmān* is to accept Allāh and the Rasūl ☺ and to surrender to Allāh. For those who accept this with absolute certitude, the second duty is to worship Him alone, without accepting any idols or images, without thinking for even a moment that there might be an equal or a partner or anyone comparable to Him. Every one of the 43,242 breaths inhaled and exhaled daily by those with such *īmān* is in *tasbīh* to Allāh, glorifying His name. Each breath is in *rukū',* bowing, and *sajdah,* prostrating, to Allāh. Their focus is on Allāh alone. Their worship is most exalted, and they are most exalted in *īmān.* They are first and foremost among those who are in *Īmān*-Islām. They have accepted that Allāh alone is sufficient for everything they need in life. Allāh is their *rahmah,* grace, their *rūh,* soul, their food, and their wealth. Such people have no other wealth. They are known as the seventy-third group.

Of the seventy-three groups of mankind who are the descendants of Adam ☺, only that one group has such perfect *īmān* and is in a state of pure Islām. Of the other seventy-two groups descended from Adam ☺, seventy have no *īmān.* and have not fulfilled the first and second *furūd.* The two remaining groups do accept and worship Allāh, but they also have a desire for the world, for earth, woman, and gold. These are the things that they love and seek to gain in life, and therefore they are selfish.

Allāh addresses these two groups in the Qur'ān: "You who have accepted *īmān!* Give charity to those who are in need, feed the hungry, take care of those with difficulties, share the *rizq,* nourishment, of Allāh with others." This third *fard,* charity, was made obligatory for those two groups of people, so that they would recognize the lives of others to be as valuable as their own. Because they could not do this correctly and did not realize the full significance of this duty, Allāhu ta'ālā, God, the Most High, ordained the fourth duty of fasting, so that they could experience the pangs of hunger and realize the sufferings of others.

For those who did not have the clarity to understand the true significance of fasting, Allāh ordained the fifth duty of *hajj*, pilgrimage to Mecca and Medina. Before undertaking the journey, they were told to give away everything they possessed and to wear a shroud like a corpse, to be dead to the world. Only then could they proceed on their pilgrimage.

Charity, fasting, and pilgrimage—these three duties were made obligatory for those who had not fully comprehended the first two duties, to have faith in God and the Rasūl ☺ and to worship God alone. However, those in the seventy-third group, for whom Allāh alone is sufficient, have nothing to give or receive. They have nothing other than Allāh, and the only gift of charity they can offer is His *rahmah*, His grace. The only things they receive from Allāh are the wisdom of the Qur'ān, the comfort of the Qur'ān, the explanations of the Qur'ān, and the *hadīth*, the traditional stories. Since these are all that they receive, these are all that they can give as charity. This seventy-third group goes directly to heaven without any judgment or reckoning, but the other two groups will be questioned on the Day of *Qiyāmah*. For them there is a Judgment Day. For the other seventy groups there is the hell of the world. The Qur'ān and the *hadīth* give evidence of this.

My brothers in Islām, beyond the five outer duties, there are the six inner *furūd*, which the Sufis have explained to us. If you go within Allāh having the certitude of *īmān*, you will see that within this eye of yours there is an inner eye which can gaze upon Allāh. Within this nostril there is a piece of flesh, a tissue which can smell the fragrance of Allāh. Within this ear there is a piece of flesh that can hear the sounds of Allāh. Within this tongue there is a piece of flesh that can taste the beauty of Allāh, taste His '*ilm*, divine knowledge, and know the taste of His *daulah*, wealth. Within this tongue there is a voice that converses with Him and recites the *dhikr*, remembrance of God, in the state of total absorption in Him. And within this *qalb*, inner heart, there is a piece of flesh where the eighteen thousand universes, Allāh's '*arsh*, throne, His *kursī*, gnostic eye, and the *qalam*, divine pen, are found. That is where the heavens, His kingdom, and His justice are all found, where the angels, the heavenly beings, the prophets, and the lights of Allāh prostrate before Him in *sajdah*. Within this piece of flesh is the palace from which He rules and passes judgment. And in that palace there is an inscription that says, "There is no God but God. He is the One who rules '*ālam*, the universe, *arwāh*, the world of the souls, and all of everything."

Within this piece of flesh is the wisdom, *hikmah*, which can discover the palace of Allāh. This is the wisdom of His '*ilm*, divine knowledge, which can be seen with perfect clarity in His Holy Qur'ān and in His holy scriptures. The clarity of this wisdom permits us to realize everything, and it is through this wisdom of '*ilm* that we can understand Him and bow down before Him. That *sajdah*, prostration, glorifies His name with each of the 43,242 daily outgoing and incoming breaths. That '*ibādah*, worship, is performed with complete knowledge.

So much is contained in the *qalb* of man, the '*arshul-mu'min*, the throne of the true believer. Within that piece of flesh inside the *qalb*, Allāh has mysteriously placed His '*arsh*, His *kursī*, and His kingdom. This is His *daulah*, wealth, and His *sirr*, secret. Only when we understand all this, will we fully understand the essence of the six inner *furūd*.

Only when a man reaches the state where he speaks to Allāh alone, can he be said to truly exist in Islām. When he attains that state of communion with Allāh, he will understand that the Qur'ān and the *kitābs,* holy books, are his own body, the *sūratul-insān.* Such a man will understand the inner meaning of *al-hamdu lillāh,* which is the praise of the *sūratul-insān.* Understanding the history of the One who is *al-hamdu lillāh,* he will praise Him alone. Only then can he understand what *'ilm* is and see this history as one continuous study, an endless ocean of divine knowledge. Otherwise, each book he reads will explain a few points and then refer him to another book, which will then refer him to yet another book. As long as he continues reading only those outer books, he will never reach his freedom.

My brothers, we must consider how the Qur'ān came from Allāh, and we must delve deep within it. In order to understand its true meaning, we must be in the same state as that original Qur'ān was when it emerged from Allāh. It came as a resplendence, a radiance, a resonance, and a grace. Then it came as a light to Gabriel ☺, and when it came to Muhammad, the Rasūl ☺, it came as the *rahmah,* grace, and *wilāyats,* attributes, of Allāh. Next Muhammad ☺ brought it to us as a *wahy,* revelation. Then the sound of these revelations was transformed into letters and formed into words. What was revealed in those words ultimately became public knowledge and part of history.

The interpretations of this knowledge later gave rise to religious differences, divisions, and bigotry, which in turn gave rise to prejudice, fighting, and wars. This is the state the world has come to. But we must delve into the depths of the Qur'ān and experience each step of the way as it originally came from Allāh. As we look deeper and deeper, we will see the Rasūl ☺, and once we see him, we will know how Gabriel ☺ came to him. We will know how the Rasūl ﷺ received that grace, and we will see the light. If we look through that light we will experience the resonance of Allāh within the Qur'ān, and as we understand that resonance, we will understand our *hayāh* and our *maut,* our life and death. We will understand the Day of Judgment, the Day of *Qiyāmah,* Questioning, and the ninety-nine *wilāyats,* attributes, of Allāh.

Once we have this understanding, we will see that all men are our brothers, just as the Qur'ān teaches us. To truly see all people as our brothers is Islām. If we see anyone who is in need, we must offer him the water of the *rahmatul-'ālamīn,* the mercy of all the universes, the water of *īmān,* and the *ash-shahādah kalimah.* That water must be given to everyone who is hungry or thirsty. We must embrace them lovingly, quench their thirst, and wash away their dirt. We must offer them love, compassion, patience, and tolerance, just as the Rasūlullāh ﷺ did. This is what will satisfy their needs and dispel the darkness in their hearts.

My brothers and sisters in Islām, if we offer peace, then justice will flourish. Love will cut away all enmity. Compassion will cause God's grace to grow in this world, and then the food of *īmān* and the *rahmatul-'ālamīn* can be offered. When that food is given, hunger, disease, old age, and death will be eliminated, and everyone will have peace.

Allāh and the state of a true *insān* are right here within us. It is a great secret, hidden within our *qalbs,* inner hearts, within the *Ummul*-Qur'ān. Only if we can study this *'ilm,* divine knowledge, can we attain our freedom. We must reflect on this. All who have *īmān* must understand this, reflect upon it, and teach it to those who have less wisdom, to those who have no clarity of heart, to those whose minds oppose us, and to those who have no peace of mind. We must teach them these qualities, give them this food, this beauty, and this nourishment of *rahmah* and *īmān.* Every human being in the community of Islām, everyone who has *īmān*, all those who are learned and wise, all the *imāms*, leaders of prayer, and *'ulamā'*, teachers, all those who know the Qur'ān—all must understand this. This is what I ask of you.

Āmīn. Āmīn. Allāh is sufficient unto us all.

CHAPTER ELEVEN

THE TRUE
MEANING
OF ISLĀM

Yā Samī'

O All-Hearing One

To all who say they believe in God, please realize with your faith that God hears every word you say. God hears your every thought. Realizing this, speak only what is truth and act only with God's qualities of love, compassion, justice, patience, and the realization that each life is as important as your own.

CHAPTER THIRTEEN

THE TRUE MEANING
OF ISLĀM

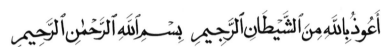

I seek refuge in Allāh from the accursed satan.
In the name of Allāh, the Most Compassionate, the Most Merciful.

May all praise be for God alone. May we give the entire responsibility for our lives to that one God who is limitless grace and incomparable love. May the peace of God and all His blessings fill the lives of all who may read this message.

To all who say they believe in God, please realize with your faith that God hears every word you say. God hears your every thought. Realizing this, speak only what is truth and act only with God's qualities of love, compassion, justice, patience, and the realization that each life is as important as your own. This is the true message within the Qur'ān. The Qur'ān does not cause divisions among God's children. It exists to bring about brotherhood and unity. The Qur'ān soothes those who weep in sorrow and gives comfort to those who suffer. To those who may be poor, it explains the bounteous wealth of God. It inspires faith in those who may not have believed in God and helps them reach a state of reverence for God.

Do not wave the words of the Qur'ān as though they were

181

a banner you were going to carry into battle. Do not say, "The Qur'ān says this and the Qur'ān says that," without truly understanding the inner wisdom of God's qualities within your own life. If one has *īmān*, faith, certitude, and determination, he will see the seed of that purity that is Islām within everything. He will see the Power of Allāh in every creation.

Therefore, he will not discriminate against another creation or discard him. Anyone who has the purity of Islām and that true *īmān* within his heart cannot hurt the heart of another in any manner. Instead, he will have *sabūr*, the patience of God, in dealing with others; he will use his *shukūr*, gratitude to God, as the strength with which to comfort others; *al-hamdu lillāh*, his praise for God, will be the wealth he will share with others; and *tawakkul*, his total trust in God, will be his own wealth, contentment, and security. He will consider anything that does not exist as the qualities of God (known in Islām as Allāh's ninety-nine names or powers) as *harām*, forbidden, or evil. Only that which exists within those divine qualities is *halāl*, permissible, or good.

These attributes of the grace of God are the law of the Qur'ān. These divine attributes are the law within the heart of one who has true *īmān* and is truly Islām. The capture of other lives and attacks against other countries are not the law. The Rasūlullāh, Muhammad, the Messenger of God ⊕ did not keep anything other than God. From the time of his appearance until the time he departed, the only wealth the Rasūlullāh ⊕ displayed and the only power he showed was the wealth and the power of God's qualities of compassion and grace.

Children of any religion who have true faith must realize that God is the only One who knows all of everything. Therefore, only God can judge whether a person has *īmān*, faith, certitude, and determination, or not and whether a person lives with that purity that can be called Islām or not. No one else can give that judgment. Do not wave your religion like a banner and go out to capture others. Only one kind of war is permissible in the eyes of God: the war you wage within yourself to defeat the demonic forces of lust, anger, jealousy, desire for revenge, and other evil feelings and attributes that may exist within your heart. God has sent each of the prophets as witnesses to the grace of God and as supports to help us in this inner war. This is the reason for the Qur'ān. It is to help the true Muslim fight this inner battle and win victory over his own *nafs,* base desires, that God sent the Messenger ☉ with the Qur'ān. We must use the wisdom contained within the Qur'ān to spank our own naughty minds and defeat our own compulsive desires. If we do that, what is called Islām will taste like honey. What we do now by battling in the world and calling it Islām tastes bitter and covers the light of the Qur'ān in darkness.

The light of Islām should reveal the essence of God in every life. If we see that essence, then we will live in unity; we will eat from the same plate; we will live as one family whether some are in a church, some are in a mosque, or some are in their homes. The beggar and the king will be able to pray together. We will discover our own faults, discard our own anger, and embrace one another with love. That is what the Qur'ān says. That is why we cannot tell lies, indulge in treachery, or threaten to kill other lives and claim that it is being done in the name of Islām. Islām teaches that we must recognize and praise the essence of God as it exists in each and every life.

Consider this explanation of the truth that is in the Qur'ān: If you take a tiny atom and split it into ten million particles and take one of these particles and examine it with that true wisdom found within Islām, you will see within that tiny particle ninety-nine particles revolving around one another without touching. (The ninety-nine are those qualities of God's grace that are known as the names or powers of God.) If you take one of those ninety-nine particles and split it into five million particles and examine one of those pieces with that wisdom, again you will see ninety-nine, ninety-nine revolving around one another without touching. And if you take any one of those particles and split it into one million pieces and examine one piece, again you will see the ninety-nine particles revolving around one another. If you take one of those and split it into five hundred thousand pieces and take one of those particles and split it into two hundred and fifty thousand pieces and take one of those and split it into one hundred thousand pieces and then one of those into ten thousand pieces and one of those into another thousand pieces and if you take one of those infinitesimal particles and look within it with that wisdom, you will see ninety-nine: His *wilāyats,* ninety-nine divine powers. Every particle of every atom contains the Power of Allāh, the Divine Power of God.

We who are Islām must realize this. If we reflect on this, anyone who calls himself Islām will never harm anyone. He will not wreak revenge. He will not be treacherous towards anyone. Islām must realize this. Everyone who has faith in God must realize this.

All children of God, leave behind all lustful desires and come to the plenitude of firm faith in God. Give up anger and come to the house of patience. Give up the tendency towards vengeance and treachery and come into the house of contentment with God's wealth of grace. Give up the hell caused by your attachment to the world and come into the love of God that is His grace. Only when you incorporate His ninety-nine compassionate powers as the basis for your actions and as the law for your life can you discover even one atom—one tiny particle—of God's mercy and compassion.

Bismillāhir-Rahmānir-Rahīm. In the name of God, the Most Compassionate, the Most Merciful. May all praise and praising be to God alone, and may we have His peace in our hearts. *Āmīn.*

EPILOGUE

Rabbul-ʿālamīn

Lord of all the universes

...Our entire life and everything that happens to us is conducted by Allāh, not by us. He is responsible for the cause and for the effect. He is the One who carries out everything. To accept this, to accept Allāh and His kingdom, is Islām. This is the birthright of the children of Adam ☾.

EPILOGUE

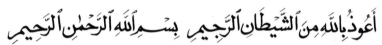

I seek refuge in Allāh from the accursed satan.
In the name of Allāh, the Most Compassionate, the Most Merciful.

As-salāmu 'alaikum wa rahmatullāhi wa barakātuhu kulluhu. May all the peace, the beneficence, and the blessings of God be upon you.

My brothers and sisters, in closing, let us reflect still further on the meaning of Islām.

The treasure of Islām is the *daulah,* the wealth of Allāh, over which He rules. Allāh is the One who protects all lives, the One who feeds and looks after all lives according to their needs and their hunger. He pacifies all hearts, giving them peace and tranquility. With His qualities of love and compassion, He rules all lives and all the universes. Islām is Allāh—His qualities, His actions, His conduct, His compassion, His peacefulness, and His unity. Islām is the kingdom of Allāh's qualities and the tranquility He gives through His peace. That plenitude is Islām.

Islām is the acceptance of Allāh as the Ruler and Master of everything. He is the Leader of all good thoughts and good qualities, the Guide for our conscience, and the One who teaches us

189

justice and truth, compassion and unity. Allāh is the Leader of all
such qualities and actions. He is the Leader of wisdom and divine
knowledge, 'ilm. That is His kingdom, and He is the only One
who rules His kingdom.

His is the kingdom of truth. What the world calls Islām cannot rule that kingdom. Man cannot rule that kingdom. In the
beginning and in the end, in life and in death, Allāh alone rules
all that is within His realm. The world and all the countries of the
world, the heart of man, the trees, plants, and houses—none of
these can be ruled by the Islām that people commonly speak of.
Allāh, not man, is the One who rules.

True Islām does not mean shouting, "I am the ruler!" and
trying to dominate the world. Allāh is the only One who rules His
kingdom. All lives, their food, and everything within that kingdom are under His rule. In this world and the next, in birth and
in death, the One who rules Islām is Allāh. No one else has the
power to govern that kingdom.

To understand this, to accept Him and His words, and to
know with absolute clarity that this is Allāh's kingdom, is to
become His 'abd, His slave. This is the way of true Islām. This is
the way of īmān and the way of the kalimah.

If we understand this, then we will realize that our entire life
and everything that happens to us is conducted by Allāh, not by
us. He is responsible for the cause and for the effect. He is the One
who carries out everything. To accept this, to accept Allāh and
His kingdom, is Islām. This is the birthright of all the children of
Adam ⊕. To acquire this 'ilm and īmān and to become His slave
is prayer. To accept His words and His commands is wisdom. To
accept what He has given us is plenitude.

Allāhu akbar. God is most great. Al-hamdu lillāh. All praise
and praising belong only to Him. Allāh is the One who gives us

the wealth of our lives. He is the One who gives us everything. Allāh is the only Leader for the kingdom of Islām. There is no other leader. Any attempt to rule that kingdom which is His benevolent, pure gift will only bring destruction. As soon as any man tries to rule the pure kingdom of Allāh, he brings about his own destruction. We, the children of Adam ☉, should know this clearly and absolutely. All those with *īmān*, who pray to Him with certitude, must think about this.

Al-hamdu lillāh! Allāhu *akbar:* This is the true meaning of Islām.

As-salāmu ʿalaikum. May the peace of God be upon you. May God help us all. *Āmīn.*

AL-KALIMATUL-KHAMS
The Five *Kalimahs*

Al-Kalimatul-Ūlā
The First *Kalimah*

Lā ilāha illAllāh, Muhammadur-Rasūlullāh.
There is no God but Allāh,
and Muhammad is the Messenger of God.

Al-Kalimatuth-Thāniya
(*Ash-Shahādah*)
The Second *Kalimah*
(The Affirmation of Faith)

*Ash-hadu al-lā ilāha illAllāhu wahdahu lā sharīka lah;
wa ash-hadu anna Muhammadan 'abduhu wa rasūluh.*
I witness that there is no God but Allāh, He is One without a
partner; I witness that Muhammad is His slave
and His Messenger.

Al-Kalimatuth-Thālithah
The Third *Kalimah*

Subhānallāhi wal-hamdu lillāhi wa lā ilāha illAllāhu
wallāhu akbar. Wa lā haula wa lā quwwata illā billāhi
wa huwal-'aliyyul-'azīm.

Glory is Allāh's, and all praise is Allāh's,
and there is no God but Allāh,
and Muhammad is the Messenger of Allāh.
And Allāh is most great! And there is no majesty
and power except in Allāh,
and He is exalted, supremely magnificent!

Al-Kalimatur-Rābi'ah
The Fourth *Kalimah*

Lā ilāha illAllāhu wahdahu lā sharīka lah;
lahul-mulku wa lahul-hamd; yuhyī wa yumīt;
biyadihil-khair; wa huwa 'alā kulli shay'in qadīr.

There is no God but Allāh,
and Muhammad is the Messenger of God.
He is One without a partner.
His is the dominion and His is the praise;
He bestows life and death, in His hand are the blessings,
and He is omnipotent over all things.

Al-Kalimatul-Khāmisah
The Fifth *Kalimah*

Allāhumma innī a'ūdhu bika min an ushrīka bīka shay'aw-
wa ana a'lam, wa astaghfiruka lima lā a'lam, innaka anta
'ālimul-ghaibi wash-shahādah. Tubtu 'anhu wa tabarra'tu 'an
kulli dīnin siwā dīnil-Islām, wa aslamtu laka wa aqūlu:
lā ilāha illAllāh, Muhammadur-Rasūlullāh.

Dearest Allāh! I seek protection in You
against ascribing any partner to You knowingly,
and I beg Your forgiveness for that which I know not of—
indeed, You are the Knower of both what is seen
and what is hidden. I have turned from such faults
and I absolve myself from every sort of creed except
pure belief in and surrender to You,
and I commit myself wholly to You saying,
"There is no God but Allāh,
and Muhammad is the Messenger of Allāh!"

GLOSSARY

The following traditional honorific phrases in Arabic calligraphy are used in the text:

⊕ *sallAllāhu 'alaihi wa sallam,* may Allāh bless him and grant him peace, is used after mentioning the name of Prophet Muhammad, the Rasūlullāh, the Messenger of Allāh.

⊛ *'alaihis-salām,* peace be upon him, is used after mentioning the name of a prophet, messenger, or angel.

⊕ *radiyAllāhu 'anhu* or *'anhā,* may Allāh be pleased with him or her, is used after mentioning the name of a companion of the Prophet Muhammad ⊕, *Qutbs,* wives of the prophets, and exalted saints.

⊕ *rahmatullāhi 'alaihi* or *'alaihā,* may the compassion of Allāh be upon him or her.

(A) Indicates an Arabic word. (P) Indicates a Persian word.
(T) Indicates a Tamil word. (H) Indicates a Hebrew word.
Note: Tamil and Arabic words that have become common usage in the English language are not italicized and those that have not become common usage are italicized. Also, proper names have not been italicized.
For simplicity's sake, we have most often used the English "s" for the plural form of foreign words.

A

'abd (A) Slave; servant.

Adōnai (H) God.

aham (T) The heart. Combining Tamil with Arabic, Bawa Muhaiyaddeen ⊕ defines Muhammad ⊕ as the *muham* (Tamil for face, *muhayyan* in Arabic) and *aham.* Thus, Muhammad ⊕ is the beauty of the heart reflected in the face.

ahmad (A) The state of the heart, the *qalb,* or *aham. Ahmad* is the heart of Muhammad ⊕. The beauty of the heart, *aham,* is the beauty of the countenance (*muham,* Tamil) of Muhammad ⊕. That is the beauty of Allāh's qualities. This is a name that comes from within the ocean of divine knowledge, *bahrul-'ilm*. Allāh is the One who is worthy of the praise of the *qalb*, the heart. Literally, most praiseworthy.

ākhirah (A) More properly *al-ākhirah*. Literally, that which exists after an appointed time; the hereafter; last day. The permanent kingdom of God, comprising both heaven and hell, that begins on the Day of Judgment; the Hereafter. Often contrasted against *ad-dunyā*, this ephemeral world. Belief in *al-ākhirah* is one of the six pillars of faith in Islām. The word appears in the Qur'ān one hundred and fifteen times. (e.g. *Sūratul-Hadīd,* 20ᵗʰ verse: "And in *al-ākhirah* is strong punishment and also forgiveness from Allāh and acceptance.")

'ālam, 'ālamīn (plural) (A) The universe, the cosmos, the metaphysical world.

al-hamdu lillāh (A) All praise is to Allāh. Allāh is the glory and greatness that deserves all praise. "You are the One responsible for the appearance of all creations. Whatever appears, whatever disappears, whatever receives benefit or loss—all is Yours. I have surrendered everything into Your hands. I remain with hands outstretched, spread out, empty, and helpless. Whatever is happening and whatever is going to happen is all Yours."

alif (A) The first letter of the Arabic alphabet, equivalent to the English letter "a." To the transformed man of wisdom, *alif* represents Allāh, the One who stands alone.

'ālim, 'ulamā' (plural) (A) Teacher; learned one; one of wisdom. One who swims in Allāh's *dhāt*, essence of grace, and has learned the ocean of divine knowledge, *bahrul-'ilm*.

Allāh, Allāhu (A) God.

Allāhu *akbar* (A) God is greater!

Allāhu ta'ālā (A) God the High, the Exalted.

Allāhu ta'ālā Nāyan (A & T) God the Exalted is the Ruler.
   Allāhu (A) The beautiful, undiminishing One; ta'ālā (A) The One who exists in all lives in a state of humility and exaltedness; Nāyan (T) The Ruler who protects and sustains.

ambiyā', nabī (singular) (A) Prophets.

āmīn (A) So be it. May He make this complete.

Amīrul-Mu'minīn (A) Commander of the faithful, a name given to
'Umar ibnul-Khattāb ☺.

Ān'ām (A) Cattle. *Al-Ān'ām* is the title of the sixth *sūrah,* chapter, of
the Qur'ān.

An'am Muhammad (A) The food; the *rizq;* the nourishment of all
creations.

Āndavan (T) God.

'arsh (A) The throne of God; the plenitude from which God rules. The
station located on the crown of the head, which is the throne that
can bear the weight of Allāh. Allāh is so heavy that we cannot carry
the load with our hands or legs. The *'arsh* is the only part of man
that can support Allāh.

'arshul-mu'min (A) The throne of the true believer; the throne
of one who has steadfast *īmān,* absolute faith, certitude, and
determination; the throne of an *insān,* a man who has that perfect
certitude of *īmān.* Allāh resides within the heart which praises
Him, the tongue which speaks only virtuous thoughts, the tongue
which speaks the truth and praises the truth.

arwāh (A) The world of pure souls, where all souls are performing
tasbīh, prayers of praise to God. Literally, souls.

'asr (A) Afternoon prayer.

as-salāmu 'alaikum (A) May the peace of God be upon you. This is the
greeting of love. *As-salāmu 'alaikum; wa 'alaikumus-salām.* One
heart embraces the other with love and greets it with respect and
honor. Both hearts are one. In reply, *wa 'alaikumus-salām* means:
May the peace of God be upon you also.

as-salāmu 'alaikum wa rahmatullāhi wa barakātahu kulluhu (A) May
all the peace, the beneficence, and the blessings of God be upon
you.

as-hāb (A) Companions of Prophet Muhammad ☺.

ash-shahādah kalimah (A) The second *kalimah,* the testimony of faith.
*Ash-hādu al-lā ilāha illAllāhu wahdahu lā sharika lah; wa ash-hādu
anna Muhammadan 'abduhu wa rasūluh*—I witness that there is
no God but Allāh; only You are God; He is One without a partner,

and I witness that Muhammad is His slave and His Messenger.

asmā'ul-husnā (A) (more properly *al-asmā' ul-husnā*) The ninety-nine beautiful names of Allāh. The plenitude of the ninety-nine duties of God; the *sifāt* of His *dhāt*, the manifestations of His essence. The states of His qualities are His manifestations which emerge from Him. He performs His duty when these manifestations of His essence are brought into action. Then they become His *wilāyats*, the actions which stem from the manifestations of His essence.

The *asmā'ul-husnā* are the ninety-nine beautiful names of His duties. They were revealed to Prophet Muhammad ⊕ in the Qur'ān, and he explained them to his followers. This is a vast *bahrud-daulat*, a very deep ocean of His grace and His limitless, infinite, and undiminishing wealth.

If we go on cutting one of these ninety-nine *wilāyats* over and over again, taking one piece at a time, we will see ninety-nine particles revolving one around the other without touching. This applies to each one of the ninety-nine *wilāyats*. This is the *asmā'ul-husnā*. As we go on cutting, we lose ourselves in that. We die within that.

How can we ever hope to reach an end of the ninety-nine? If we receive only one drop of that, it will be more than sufficient for us. The person who has touched the smallest, tiniest drop becomes a good one. These are merely His powers. If you go on cutting just one of His powers, it is so powerful that it will draw you in. That Power will swallow you up, and you become the power, *wilāyat*. Then you come to the stage at which you can lose yourself within Allāh; you can disappear within Allāh.

'asr (A) The third of the five times prayers; also means era, time, and afternoon.

astaghfirullāhal-'aliyyal-'azīm (A) I ask Allāh, the Exalted and Supreme, for forgiveness.

a'ūdhu billāhi minash-shaitānir-rajīm (A) I seek refuge in God from the accursed satan.

auliyā', walī (singular) (A) The favorites of God. Those who are near to God, referring to holy men and women of Islām.

awwal (A) More properly *al-awwal.* Literally, the first. The state in which forms begin to manifest; the beginning of time and space; the stage at which the soul became surrounded by form and each creation took shape; the stage at which the souls of the six kinds of lives (earth life, fire life, water life, air life, ether life, and light life) were placed in their respective forms. Allāh created these forms and then placed that "trust property" which is life within those forms.

Awwal Muhammad (A) The Beginning. *Awwal* is the beginning, the emergence of creation. At this time Allāh gave the name *Awwal Muhammad* to the Light of the *Nūr.*

āyah, āyats (plural) (A) A verse in the Qur'ān; a sign or miracle.

B

bahr (A) Ocean.

bahrul-'ilm (A) The ocean of divine knowledge.

al-Baitul-Muqaddas: The original temple in Jerusalem over which is now built the Masjidul-Aqsā' and near which site the Dome of the Rock stands today. Al-Baitul-Muqaddas was where the Prophet ☉ was first taken in the *mi'rāj;* then he ascended on *Burāq* from the site of the Qubbatus-Sakhrah, the Dome of the Rock.

barakah, barakāt (plural) (A) The wealth of Allāh's grace. Literally, blessing.

Bismillāhir-Rahmānir-Rahīm (A) In the name of God, the Most Compassionate, the Most Merciful. *Bismillāh:* Allāh is the first and the last, the One with the beginning and without beginning. He is the One who is the cause for creation and for the absence of creation, the cause for the beginning and for the beginningless. *Ar-Rahmān:* He is the King, the Nourisher, the One who gives food. He is the Compassionate One. He is the One who protects the creations. He is the Beneficent One. *Ar-Rahīm:* He is the One who redeems, the One who protects from evil, who preserves and who confers eternal bliss; the Savior. On the Day of Judgment and on the Day of Inquiry and on all days from the day of the beginning, He protects and brings His creations back unto Himself.

D

dahūt (P) Throne.

dajjal (A) Antichrist. Literally, lying, false.

daulah (A) Wealth. This has two meanings. One is the wealth of
the world, *dunyā*. The other is the wealth of the grace of Allāh.
The wealth of Allāh is the wealth of *'ilm*, divine knowledge,
and the wealth of perfect *īmān*, absolute faith, certitude, and
determination. Literally, dynasty, state, power, country, empire;
change, rotation, alternation, and change of fortune.

dhāt (A) The essence of God; His treasury; His wealth of purity; His
grace.

dhikr (A) The remembrance of God. It is a common name given
to certain words in praise of God. Of the many *dhikrs,* the most
exalted *dhikr* is to say, "*Lā ilāha illAllāhu.* There is nothing other
than You. Only You are Allāh." All the others relate to His *wilāyats,*
actions, but this *dhikr* points to Him and to Him alone.

dīn (A) The light of perfect purity; the resplendence of perfectly
pure *īmān,* absolute faith, certitude, and determination. Literally,
religion, faith, belief.

*dīnul-*Islām (A) The path of perfect purity; the resplendence of
absolute certitude of faith, *īmān;* the ancient truth that was in Allāh
originally and is always with Him. The light of truth for *dunyā,* the
world, and *ākhirah,* the hereafter. For those who dwell within it,
*dīnul-*Islām is the faith of unquestioning surrender to the will of
Allāh.

du'ā' (A) A prayer of supplication.

du'ā'u barakah (A) A supplicatory prayer for the blessing of Allāh.

dunyā (A) The world; the world of physical existence; the darkness
which separated from Allāh at the time when the Light of the *Nūr
Muhammad* manifested from within Allāh.

F

fard, furūd (plural) (A) An obligatory duty.

fikr (A) Contemplation, meditation, concentration on God.

firdaus (A) The eighth heaven. If we can cut away the seven base desires known as the *nafs ammārah,* what remains will be Allāh's qualities, actions, and conduct, His gracious attributes, and His duties. If man can make these his own and store them within his heart, then that is *firdaus.* That is Allāh's house, the limitless heaven. That will be the eighth heaven, Allāh's house of infinite magnitude and perfect purity.

furūd, fard (singular) (A) The five *furūd* refer to the five pillars of Islām: *īmān,* or absolute faith in God (as reflected in the *shahādah, ash-hadu al-lā ilāha illAllāh, wa ash-hadu anna Muhammadar-Rasūlullāh,* meaning, "I witness that there is no God but Allāh, and I witness that Muhammad is the Messenger of Allāh"), prayer, charity, fasting, and *hajj,* pilgrimage.

G

gnānam (T) Divine luminous wisdom; grace-awakened wisdom. If man can throw away all the worldly treasures and take within him only the Treasure called Allāh and His qualities and actions, His conduct and behavior, if he makes Allāh the only Treasure and Completeness for him—that is the state of *gnānam.*

gnāni (T) A wise man; a man of divine wisdom.

H

hadīth (A) In Islām, a traditional story spoken by the prophets. These are the words or commands of Allāh which were received by Prophet Muhammad ⊕ and the other prophets, and were then conveyed and demonstrated to the people. Words of wisdom; sometimes a story about the prophets.

hadīth qudsī (A) A divine transmission directly revealed to Prophet Muhammad ⊕ without Gabriel ⊚ as an intermediary.

haif (A) Wrong, injustice, prejudice, harmful, damaging.

hajj (A) The holy pilgrimage to Mecca; the fifth *fard,* obligatory duty, in Islām. This duty must be done wearing the white shroud, *kafan,* of one who has died to the world. Before you undertake this pilgrimage, you must share your wealth among the poor. If you have a spouse and children, you must divide your wealth among them.

True pilgrimage is to enter the state of dying before death. The
inner desires must be surrendered and all of the self must die to
make this pilgrimage.

halāl (A) That which is permissible or lawful according to the
commands of God and which conforms to the word of God. This
relates to both food and to divine knowledge, *'ilm.*

harām (A) That which is forbidden by truth and forbidden by the
warnings or commands of God. For those who are on the straight
path, *harām* means all the evil things, the actions, the food, and the
dangers that can obstruct the path.

harf (A) A letter of the alphabet.

hayāh (A) The plenitude of man's eternal life; the splendor of the
completeness of life; the *rūh,* soul, of the splendor of man's life.

Hayāt Muhammad (A) The eternal; the *rūh,* soul, or life, which exists
forever; the truth which never dies.

hikmah (A) Divine wisdom.

I

'ibādah (A) Worship and service to the one God.

ihsān (A) To do right and to act beautifully, because one knows that
God is always watching man's actions and thoughts.

illAllāhu (A) Only You are Allāh; You alone exist. The second half of
the *dhikr, lā ilāha illAllāhu.*

'ilm (A) Allāh's divine knowledge.

imām (A) A leader of prayer.

īmān (A) Absolute, complete, and unshakable faith, certitude, and
determination that God alone exists; the complete acceptance of
the heart that God is One.

Īmān-Islām (A) Perfect certitude and purity of faith in Allāh; the state
of the spotlessly pure heart which contains Allāh's Holy Qur'ān,
His divine radiance, His divine wisdom, His truth, His prophets,
His angels, and His laws. When the resplendence of Allāh is seen as
the completeness within this pure heart of man, that is *Īmān-Islām.*
When the complete, unshakable faith of this pure heart is directed
towards the One who is Completeness and is made to merge with
that One; when that heart trusts only in Him and worships only

Him, accepting Him as the only perfection and the only One worthy of worship—that is *Īmān*-Islām.

insān (A) Man; a true human being.

insān kāmil (A) A pure human being or perfected or completed God-realized human being. One who has realized Allāh as his only wealth, cutting away the wealth of the world and the wealth sought by the mind. One who has acquired God's qualities, performs his own actions accordingly, and immerses himself within those qualities. One in whom everything other than Allāh has been extinguished.

in shā'Allāh (A) If God has willed.

Islām (A) Purity; unity; the state of total and unconditional surrender to the will of God; the state of absolute purity; to accept the commands of God and His qualities and actions and to establish that state of purity within oneself, worshipping Him alone.

J

jihād (A) Literally, holy war. Bawa Muhaiyaddeen ☺ explains that the holy wars that the children of Adam ☺ are waging today are not true holy wars. Praising Allāh and then destroying others is not *jihād*. Allāh has no thought of killing other lives or going to war. For man to kill another man is not *jihād*. We will have to answer for that kind of *jihād* when we are questioned in the grave. True *jihād* is to praise God and cut away the satanic enemies and evil desires within our own selves. To wage war and cut our connection to this inner enemy that is leading us to hell is true *jihād*.

jum'ah (A) In Islām, the traditional gathering for prayers on Friday, at midday.

juz' (A) Part, portion, section. The Holy Qur'ān contains thirty *juz'*.

K

Ka'bah (A) In Islām, the Ka'bah is the most important shrine for worship. The place where the earlier prophets and the Final Prophet, Muhammad ☺ gathered together in prayer. On the path of *sharī'ah,* one of the five obligations, *furūd,* is the pilgrimage to the Ka'bah known as *hajj.*

Another meaning: the inner heart, *qalb,* which is the original source of prayer; the place where *insān,* man, meets Allāh face to face. Whoever brings his heart to that state of perfection and prays to God from that heart will be praying from the Ka'bah.

kāfir (A) One who rejects faith in Allāh; one who is ungrateful for the blessings of Allāh. Literally, unbeliever; infidel.

kalimah (A) *Lā ilāha illAllāhu:* There is nothing other than You, O God. Only You are Allāh.

The recitation or remembrance of God which cuts away the influence of the five elements (earth, fire, water, air, and ether), washes away all the karma that has accumulated from the very beginning until now, dispels the darkness, beautifies the heart, and causes it to resplend.

The *kalimah* washes the body and the heart of man and makes them pure, makes his wisdom emerge, and impels that wisdom to know the self and God.

kāmil (A) Perfect, perfect one, complete or finished.

kastūrī (T) The fragrance of the beautiful qualities of Allāh. Literally, a musk fragrance.

khair (A) That which is right or good; that which is acceptable to wisdom and to Allāh, as opposed to *sharr,* that which is evil or bad.

kitāb (A) Book.

kufr (A) The rejection of faith in Allāh after understanding the truth. Not believing in Allāh, the Rasūl ☉, and the Qur'ān; infidelity. Literally, that which covers the truth; ingratitude.

kursī (A) The gnostic eye; the eye of light; the center of the forehead where the Light of Allāh's *Nūr,* His resplendence, was impressed on the forehead of Adam ☉. Literally, chair, seat, throne.

L

lā ilāha illAllāhu (A) "There is nothing other than You, O God. Only You are God." There is only one Lord, one deity, one God. To accept this with certitude, to strengthen one's *īmān,* absolute faith, and to affirm this *kalimah* is the state of Islām.

There are two aspects: *Lā ilāha* is the manifestation of creation, *sifāt. IllAllāhu* is the essence, *dhāt.* All that has appeared,

all creation, belongs to *lā ilāha*. The One who created all that, His
name is *illAllāhu*. Literally, there is no God but Allāh.

lā ilāha illAllāh Muhammadur-Rasūlullāh (A) There is no God but
Allāh, and Muhammad is the Messenger of God.

lām (A) A letter in the Arabic alphabet, corresponding to the English
consonant "l," which stands, within the realm of wisdom, for the
Nūr, Light, the Light of wisdom.

la'natul-jahannam (A) The curse of hell.

lebbe (A) One who does service in a mosque.

M

maghrib (A) The fourth *waqt* of the five times prayer in Islām.
Literally, the time of sunset; also means the west.

mahr (A) A dowry or settlement of money or property on a wife,
without which a marriage is not legal.

malā'ikah, malak (singular) (A) Archangels. Literally, angels.

malak (A) Angel.

ma shā'Allāh (A) Whatever God has willed.

maulā (A) Literally, lord, master.

maulal-Islām (A) Allāh alone is the *Maulā*, the Lord, the Master in
Islām.

maut (A) Death.

maya (T) Illusion; the unreality of the visible world; the glitters seen in
the darkness of illusion.

mayyit (A) Corpse.

mīm (A) A letter in the Arabic alphabet, corresponding to the English
consonant "m," which stands, within the realm of wisdom, for
Muhammad ⊕ or the pure soul.

mi'rāj (A) The night journey of the Prophet Muhammad ⊕ through
the heavens said to have taken place in the twelfth year of the
Prophet's mission, on the twenty-seventh month of *Rajāb*. During
this event the divine order for five times prayer was given. Literally,
an ascent.

miskīn (A) A poor person, one who possesses no property at all.

mizān (A) Balance, scale of justice.

mubārakāt (T & A) The blessings for the three worlds; Allāh's

supreme, imperishable treasures for all three worlds; *mu* (T) is
a prefix meaning three; *barakāt* (A) means blessings. Hence, the
blessings for all three worlds.

Muhaiyaddeen ☺ (A) The pure resplendence of the *Qutb* ☺. The one
who manifests the wisdom which lies hidden and buried under
illusion, maya. The one who gives life to that wisdom and shows
it again as a resplendence. The one who revives the life of wisdom
and gives it to someone else.

    Muhaiyaddeen ☺: *Mu* is that which existed earlier; *hayy* is
life, *yā* is a title of greatness, a title of praise; and *dīn* means the
Light which is perfectly pure. *Dīn* is what existed in the beginning,
the "ancient thing" which was with God originally and is always
with Him. To that purity God gave the name Muhaiyaddeen ☺.
Muhaiyaddeen ☺ is that beauty which manifested from Allāh and
to which Allāh gave His *wilāyats*, powers. Literally, the giver of life
to the true belief.

muham (T) Face or countenance. In combining Tamil with Arabic,
Bawa Muhaiyaddeen ☺ defines Muhammad ☺ as *muham* and
aham, the face and the heart, the beauty of Allāh's countenance, or
the beauty of the heart as reflected in the face.

Muhammad Mustāfār-Rasūl ☺ (A) Mustāfā—the chosen one;
ar-Rasūl—the Messenger. A name used for Prophet Muhammad ☺.

mu'min (A) A true believer; one of true *īmān*, absolute faith, certitude,
and determination.

N

nabī, ambiyā' (plural) (A) Prophet.

nafs or *nafs ammārah* (A) The seven kinds of base desires. That is,
desires meant to satisfy one's own pleasure and comforts. All
thoughts are contained within the *ammārah*. *Ammārah* is like the
mother while the *nafs* are like the children. Literally, person; spirit;
inclination or desire which goads or incites towards evil.

nuqtah, nuqat (plural) (A) A dot; a dot placed over or under certain
Arabic letters to differentiate one from another; also used in text to
mean a singular dot.

Nūr Muhammad (A) The beauty of the qualities and actions of the *wilāyats,* powers, of Allāh, the Light of Allāh's *dhāt,* essence, which shines within the resplendence of His truth. It was the Light of Muhammad ☺ called *Nūr Muhammad* that was impressed upon the forehead of Adam ☺. Of the nine aspects of Muhammad ☺, *Nūr Muhammad* is that aspect which is the wisdom.

O

oli (T) Light; one who has realized the state of *īmān,* faith, certitude, and determination; one who has disappeared within the resplendence of Allāh, shining and radiating without the least trace of fault or blemish.

P

pahut arivu (T) Divine analytic wisdom; the sixth of the seven levels of wisdom. Muhaiyaddeen ☺ ; the wisdom of Allāh that explains His mysteries to the soul. This explanation is the Qur'ān.

Q

qalam (A) The pen with which God is said to have prerecorded the actions of men. The Prophet Muhammad ☺ said that the first thing that God created was the pen, *qalam,* and that it wrote down the quantity of every individual thing to be created, all that was and all that will be to all eternity. Literally, a reed pen.

qalb (A) Heart, the heart within the heart of man, the inner heart. Bawa Muhaiyaddeen ☺ explains that there are two states for the *qalb.* One state is made up of four chambers, which represent Hinduism, Fire Worship, Christianity, and Islam. Inside these four chambers there is a flower, the flower of the *qalb* which is the divine qualities of Allāh. This is the second state, the flower of grace, *rahmat.* God's fragrance exists within this inner *qalb.*

qiblah (A) The direction one faces in prayer. For Muslims, the *qiblah* is Mecca. For Jews, it is Jerusalem. Internally, it is the throne of God within the heart, *qalb.*

Qiyāmah (A) The standing forth; the Day of Questioning or Reckoning.

Qudrah (A) The Power of God's grace and the qualities which control all other forces.

Qur'ān (A) The words of Allāh that were revealed to His Messenger, Prophet Muhammad ☺; those words that came from Allāh's Power are called the Qur'ān; Allāh's inner book of the heart; the Light of Allāh's grace which comes as a resonance from Allāh.

qurbān (A) Inwardly, it is to purify one's heart, *qalb*, by sacrificing and cutting away the animal qualities existing within oneself, thus making one's life *halāl,* permissible. The *subhānallāhi kalimah* is recited for the purpose of destroying these animal qualities within the *qalb.* Outwardly, it is the ritual method for the slaughter of animals to make them *halāl* to eat.

Qutb ☺ (A) Divine analytic wisdom, the wisdom which explains; that which measures the length and breadth of the seven oceans of the *nafs,* base desires; that which awakens all the truths which have been destroyed and buried in the ocean of maya; that which awakens true *īmān,* absolute faith, certitude, and determination; that which explains to the *hayāh,* life, the state of purity as it existed in *awwal,* the beginning of creation; the grace of the *dhāt,* the essence of God, which awakens the *hayāh* of purity and transforms it into the divine vibration. *Qutb* is also a name which has been given to Allāh. He can be addressed as *Yā Qutb* or *Yā Quddūs,* the Holy One. *Quddūs* is His *wilāyah,* His Power or miracle, while *Qutb* is His action. *Wilāyah* is the Power of that action. Literally, axis, axle, pole, pivot. Also, a title used for the great holy men of Islām.

R

Rabb (A) God; the Lord; the Creator and Protector.

Rahīm (A) God, the Most Merciful.

Rahmān (A) God, the Most Compassionate. He is the *Rahmān.* He is the King. He is the Nourisher, the One who gives food. He is the Compassionate One. He is the One who protects the creations. He is the Beneficent One.

rahmah (A) God's grace; His benevolence; His wealth. All the good things that we receive from God are called His *rahmah.* It is the wealth of God's plenitude.

Rahmatul-'ālamīn (A) The Mercy or Grace of all the universes. The

One who gives everything to all His creations.

Rasūl ⊕ (A) The Prophet Muhammad ⊕. Allāh's Rasūl ⊕ is His *dhāt*,
that is, the resplendence that emerged from His effulgence, shining
radiantly as His Messenger. The manifestation of that resplendence
discourses on the explanations of luminous wisdom which he
imparts to Allāh's creations. He is the one who begs for truth from
Allāh and intercedes with prayers, *du'ā's*, for all of Allāh's creations
and for his followers. Therefore, Allāh has anointed His Rasūl ⊕
with this title: The Messenger who is the savior for both worlds.
Literally, the word *rasūl* can be used to refer to any of Allāh's
apostles or messengers.

Rasūlullāh ⊕ (A) Prophet Muhammad ⊕, the Messenger of God.

rizq (A) Nourishment, food, sustenance, livelihood.

All that we eat is just straw and hay for desire, *nafs*. The atom
of nourishment from God is but one, and that is the *rizq*, the food
for *īmān*, absolute faith, certitude, and determination. That food
is the beauty that comes directly form Allāh. What you strip away
and discard from *rizq* is desire, *'ishq*. That food that came from
Allāh as nourishment is *rizq*. *'Ishq* is desire; that is the world.

rūh (A) The soul; the light ray of God; the light of God's wisdom,
Bawa Muhaiyaddeen ⊕ explains *rūh* to also mean *hayāh*, life. Of
the six kinds of lives, the soul is the light-life, the ray of the Light
of *Nūr*, the resplendence of Allāh, which does not die. It does not
disappear; it is the truth; it exists forever. That is the soul, the light-
life.

rukū' (A) A posture in the daily formal *salāh*, prayer, of Islām. A
bending over from the torso, with head down and hands resting on
knees.

S

sabūr (A) Patience; inner patience; to go within patience, to accept it,
to think and reflect within it. *Sabūr* is that patience deep within
patience which comforts and soothes, and alleviates mental
suffering. Literally, *sabūr* is the intensive form of *sabr*, or patience.

sadaqah (A) Charity, almsgiving, contributions to the poor.

saivam (T) Purity. It also means vegetarianism.

sajdah (A) In the *salāh,* the formal prayer of Islām, *sajdah* is a position of prostration on hands and knees, with the forehead touching the ground.

salām (A) The peace of God; greetings of peace. There are many meanings to the word *salām.* When we say *salām,* it means in God's name or in the presence of God, both of us become one without any division; both of us are in a state of unity, a state of peace.

salāh, salawāt (plural) (A) Ritual prayer, blessing.

salawāt (A) Prayers or blessings; usually used for the supplications asking God to bless the prophets and mankind.

sallallāhu ʿalaihi wa sallam (A) May the blessing and peace of Allāh be upon him. A supplication traditionally spoken after mentioning the name of Prophet Muhammad ☻. Most often abbreviated with a calligraphic circle: ☻.

saum (A) Fasting.

sayyid (A) Descendant of Prophet Muhammad ☻.

Shaikh (A) The Guru; the teacher who takes the disciples to the shore of the heart; a spiritual teacher.

shakti (T) Primal force or energy; the energy of the five elements.

sharīʿah, tarīqah, haqīqah, maʿrifah, sūfiyyah (A) The five steps of spiritual ascendance.

sharīʿah–the discrimination between good and evil and the conducting of one's life according to the good. Literally, the way that leads to water.

tarīqah–unswerving and complete acceptance of the good, and the carrying out of every action accordingly. The truth of intention, certitude, determination, faith, patience, and duty. Literally, the path.

haqīqah–the realization of Truth which is the divinity, and the beginning of communication with God.

maʿrifah–the knowledge of the secrets of God. Maʿrifah has no day or night; it is the realization of God mingled within all lives as the Light without shadow, as the Truth within truth, as the Unique One shining without separation in all the worlds.

sūfiyyah–the fifth and ultimate level of spiritual ascendance. It is the state of one who has transcended the four religions and merged with God.

sharr (A) That which is wrong, bad, or evil, as opposed to *khair* or that which is good.

shukūr (A) Gratitude; contentment with whatever may happen, realizing that everything comes from Allāh; contentment arising from gratitude.

siddhi (T) Occult power, miracle; the ability to perform miracles acquired by devotion to and control of the elements.

sifāh, sifāt (plural) (A) Form, creation, manifestation.

sirr (A) The secret of Allāh.

subhānahu wa ta'ālā (A) All glory and exaltedness is His! A spontaneous outpouring of love from a believer's heart upon hearing or uttering the name Allāh.

sunnah (A) A term used by Muslims to express the custom or manner of life, hence the tradition which records either the saying or doings of Muhammad ☮. Literally, a path or way; a manner of life.

sūrah, surāts (plural) (A) A chapter of the Qur'ān (when the initial letter is the Arabic letter *sīn*).

sūrah, surāts (plural) (A) Form or shape, such as the form of man (when the initial letter is the Arabic letter *sād*).

*sūratul-*Adam (A) The form of Adam ☮.

sūratul-insān (A) The inner form of man. The inner form of man is the Qur'ān and is linked together by the twenty-eight letters. This form, *sūrah*, is the *Ummul-*Qur'ān, the source of the Qur'ān. It is the Qur'ān in which the revelations of Allāh are revealed. The sounds in the Qur'ān which resonate through wisdom, the Messenger of Allāh, Prophet Muhammad ☮, the angels, and heavenly beings—all are made to exist in this body as secrets.

T

takbīr (A) To say Allāhu *akbar* (God alone is great. Nothing else is). This is the first *takbīr,* or exaltation of Allāh, in prayer, *salāh,* which is said standing, after which the worshipper must give himself up entirely to the remembrance of Allāh.

tārahan, singhan, and *sūran* (T) The three sons of illusion, related to aspects of the sexual act.

tasbīh (A) Glorification of God; the *subhānallāhi kalimah.* Literally, saying, "*Subhānallāh,* glory is God's."

taubah (A) Repentance; to ask forgiveness from God for sins and errors, to turn away from them, and to vow never to commit them again.

tauhīd (A) The affirmation of the unity of Allāh, the principal tenet of Islām.

tawakkul, tawakkulun 'alAllāh (A) Absolute trust and surrender; handing over to God the entire responsibility for everything. Also, *tawakkalnā 'alAllāh,* we surrender to God (first person plural form). Literally, to place your trust in Allāh.

Tiru Marai (T) The Original Qur'ān; the Inner Qur'ān inscribed within the heart. All the *sirr* and the *dhāt,* the secrets and the essence, from the three worlds of *awwal, dunyā,* and *ākhirah,* the beginning of creation, the physical world, and the hereafter, have been buried and concealed within the Qur'ān by Allāh. There He has concealed the explanations of the *dhāt,* the essence of grace, and of the manifestations of creation, *sifāt.* There He has concealed the *alif, lām,* and *mīm;* these three are the *dhāt.* That is why it is called the *Tiru* Qur'ān. *Tiru* means triple in Tamil.

tolulai (T) Most often refers to the ritual five-times prayer in Islām. Literally, worship, prayer.

U

'ulamā', 'ālim (singular) (A) Teachers, learned ones, scholars.

ummī (A) A title given to Muhammad ⊕ and found in *Sūrah* VIII of the Holy Qur'ān. Literally, one who is unlearned, illiterate.

*Ummul-*Qur'ān (A) The source or mother of the Qur'ān. It is used commonly to refer to the *Sūratul-Fātihah,* or the opening chapter of the Qur'ān. It is said that the within 124 letters of the *Sūratul-Fātihah* is contained the meaning of the entire Qur'ān. It is often used to denote the eternal source of all the revelations to all of the prophets and is also known as the *Ummul-Kitāb,* the mother, or source of the book. This is a divine, indestructible tablet on which all is recorded. This is the silent Qur'ān which exists as a mystery within the *qalb*, heart, of each person.

W

wa 'alaikumus-salam (A) And may the peace of God be upon you also.

wahy (A) Revelation; inspiration from God; the inspired word of God revealed to a prophet; the commandments or words of God. *Wahys*, revelations, have come to Adam ☺, Moses ☺, and various other prophets, but most of all to Prophet Muhammad ☺. Muhammad ☺ received 6,666 revelations. The histories of each of the prophets were contained within the revelations given to Prophet Muhammad ☺.

walī, auliyā' (plural) (A) Saint in the service of Allāh.

waqt (A) Time; time of prayer. In Islām there are five specified *waqts*, times of prayer, each day. But truly, there is only one *waqt*. That is the prayer that never ends, where one is in direct communication with God and one is merged with God.

wilāyah, wilāyats (plural) (A) God's Power; that which has been revealed and manifested through God's actions; the ninety-nine beautiful names and actions of God.

Y

Yā (A) A title of praise; a title of greatness and glory; the vocative 'O'.

Yahweh (H) God, Jehovah.

yuga (T) An age; one of the four ages of the world. According to Bawa Muhaiyaddeen ☺ the world has been in existence two hundred million years and is divided into four yugas of fifty million years each.

Z

zakāh (A) Charity.

INDE

Passim denotes that the references are scattered throughout the pages indicated *(e.g., 102-107 passim).*

ABOUT
M. R. BAWA MUHAIYADDEEN ﴿رضـﮧ﴾

The teachings of Muhammad Raheem Bawa Muhaiyaddeen ﴿رضـﮧ﴾ express the mystical explanation, the SUFI path of esoteric Islam; namely that the human being is uniquely created with the faculty of Wisdom, enabling one to trace consciousness back to its origin—Allah, the one divine Being, the Creator of all—and to surrender the self within that Source, leaving the One God, the Truth, as the only reality in one's life. He spoke endlessly of this Truth through parables, discourses, songs and stories, all pointing the way to return to God.

People from all religions and races flocked to hear and be near him; he taught everyone, regardless of origin, with love, compassion and acceptance. An extraordinary being, he taught from experience, having traversed the Path, and returned, divinely aware—sent back to exhort all who yearn for the experience of God to discover this internal Wisdom, the path of surrender to that One.

M. R. Bawa Muhaiyaddeen's known history begins in Sri Lanka. He was discovered in the pilgrimage town of Kataragama by spiritual seekers from the northern city of Jaffna. Begging him to come teach them, he did so for forty years until 1971, when he accepted an American invitation to Philadelphia, from where he lovingly taught until his passing in December, 1986.

In these distressing times, his teachings are increasingly recognized as representing the original intention of Islam which is Purity—the relationship between man and God as explained by all the prophets of God, from Adam to Noah, Abraham, Moses, Jesus and Muhammad, may the peace of God be upon them—all sent to tell and retell mankind that there is one and only one God, and that this One is their source, attainable, and waiting for the return of each individual soul.

The Bawa Muhaiyaddeen Fellowship is in Philadelphia, PA, which was the home of M. R. Bawa Muhaiyaddeen ☺ when he lived in the United States. The Fellowship continues to serve as a meeting house, as a reservoir of people and materials for everyone wishing access to his teachings.

The Mosque of Shaikh M. R. Bawa Muhaiyaddeen is located on the same property; here the five daily prayers and Friday congregational prayers are observed. An hour west of the Fellowship is the Mazār, the resting place of M. R. Bawa Muhaiyaddeen ☺ which is open daily between sunrise and sunset.

If you would like to visit the Fellowship, or to obtain a schedule of current events, branch locations and meetings, please contact:

The Bawa Muhaiyaddeen Fellowship
5820 Overbrook Avenue
Philadelphia, Pennsylvania 19131

Phone: **(215) 879-6300**
or **(215) 879-8604** (voice mail)
Fax: **(215) 879-6307**

E-mail: **info@bmf.org**
Website: **www.bmf.org**

Books in Print by
M. R. Bawa Muhaiyaddeen (ﺭﺽ)

Sūratur-Rahmah: The form of Compassion

God's Psychology: A Sufi Explanation

The Point Where God and Man Meet

The Map of the Journey to God: Lessons from the School of Grace

The Golden Words of a Sufi Sheikh, Revised Edition

Islam and World Peace: Explanations of a Sufi, Second Edition

A Book of God's Love

The Resonance of Allah: Resplendent Explanations
Arising from the *Nūr, Allāh's* Wisdom of Grace

The Tree That Fell to the West: Autobiography of a Sufi

Asmā'ul Husnā: The 99 Beautiful Names of Allah

Questions of Life—Answers of Wisdom (Vols. 1, 2)

The Fast of Ramadan: The Inner Heart Blossoms

Hajj: The Inner Pilgrimage

The Triple Flame: The Inner Secrets of Sufism

A Song of Muhammad (ﷺ)

To Die Before Death: The Sufi Way of Life

A Mystical Journey

Sheikh and Disciple

Why Can't I See the Angels:
Children's Questions to a Sufi Saint

Treasures of the Heart: Sufi Stories for Young Children

Come to the Secret Garden: Sufi Tales of Wisdom

My Love You My Children:
101 Stories for Children of All Ages

Maya Veeram or The Forces of Illusion

God, His Prophets and His Children

Four Steps to Pure *Iman*

(continued on next page)

The Wisdom of Man

Truth & Light: Brief Explanations

Songs of God's Grace

The Guidebook to the True Secret of the Heart (Vols. 1, 2)

The Divine Luminous Wisdom That Dispels the Darkness

Wisdom of the Divine (Vols. 1–6)

The Tasty, Economical Cookbook (Vols. 1, 2)

Booklets

GEMS OF WISDOM SERIES:

Vol. 1: The Value of Good Qualities
Vol. 2: Beyond Mind and Desire
Vol. 3: The Innermost Heart
Vol. 4: Come to Prayer

Pamphlets

Advice to Prisoners

Du'ā' Kanzul-'Arsh (The Invocation of the Treasure of the Throne)

Faith

The Golden Words of a Sufi Sheikh: Preface to the Book

In Commemoration of the Sixth Anniversary of the Opening of
The Mosque of Shaikh M. R. Bawa Muhaiyaddeen ☺

Islam & World Peace: Explanations of a Sufi – Jihād, The Holy War Within

Islam & World Peace: Explanations of a Sufi – The True Meaning of Islām
and Epilogue

Islam and World Peace: Explanations of a Sufi – Two Discourses

Letter to the World Family

Love is the Remedy, God Is the Healer

Marriage

The Pond – A Letter to the Fellowship Family

A Prayer for Father's Day

A Prayer for My Children

A Prayer from My Heart

Strive for a Good Life

Sufi: A Brief Explanation

A Sufi Perspective on Business

25 Duties – The True Meaning of Fellowship

With Every Breath, Say *Lā Ilāha Ill-Allāhu*

Who Is God?

Why Man Has No Peace (from My Love You, My Children)

Why We Recite the Maulids

The Wisdom and Grace of the Sufis

A CONTEMPORARY SUFI SPEAKS:

To Teenagers and Parents

On the Signs of Destruction

On Peace of Mind

On the True Meaning of Sufism

On Unity: The Legacy of the Prophets

The Meaning of Fellowship

Mind, Desire, and the Billboards of the World

FOREIGN LANGUAGE PUBLICATIONS

Ein Zeitgenössischer Sufi Spricht über Inneren Frieden
(A Contemporary Sufi Speaks on Peace of Mind—
German translation)

Deux Discours tirés du Livre L'Islam et la Paix Mondiale:
Explications d'un Soufi
(Two Discourses from the Book, Islam and World Peace:
Explanations of a Sufi—French translation)

¿Quién es Dios? Una Explicatión por el Sheikh Sufi
(Who is God? An Explanation by the Sufi Sheikh—
Spanish translation)

Other Publications

Bawa Muhaiyaddeen Fellowship Calendar

Inner & Universal Meanings of Islam
(An article about M. R. Bawa Muhaiyaddeen ㉾ and Islam:
Reprinted from the Harvard Divinity Bulletin.)

Al-hamdu lillāh!
All praise belongs to God!
Any errors or omissions are ours.

1141919

Made in the USA